THE
Hold Me
Tight

....

WORKBOOK

A COUPLE'S GUIDE FOR
A LIFETIME OF LOVE

Dr. Sue Johnson

Little, Brown Spark
New York Boston London

Little, Brown Spark
Hachette Book Group
1290 Avenue of the Americas
New York
NY 10104

littlebrownspark.com

First Edition: December 2022

Little, Brown Spark is an imprint of Little, Brown and Company, a division of Hachette Book Group, Inc. The Little, Brown Spark name and logo are trademarks of Hachette Book Group, Inc.

The publisher is not responsible for websites (or their content) that are not owned by the publisher.

The Hachette Speakers Bureau provides a wide range of authors for speaking events. To find out more, go to hachettespeakersbureau.com or call (866) 376-6591.

Library of Congress Control Number is available at the Library of Congress.

Printing 2, 2023

ISBN 9780316440233

LSC-C

Printed in the United States of America

CONTENTS

THE
Hold Me
Tight
WORKBOOK

....

Your Love Can Make Sense Again

A cross human history, the consensus has generally been that romantic love is, and always will be, a mystery—something by its very nature unknowable. Perhaps because love seems so baffling and unruly, our culture appears to be losing all faith in the viability of stable romantic partnerships. Skepticism and pessimism regarding long-term love have always been with us. But now I think we can agree that those feelings have been compounded by a new kind of stress—one we've never known before now—the stress of the COVID-19 pandemic and its aftermath, a world in a state of flux.

The time of lockdown and recovery has affected relationships of all kinds. For some couples, it was a time of coming together, regrouping, and reconnection. For others, close confinement, uncertainty, and managing virtual work and school put a strain on already fragile bonds.

As a clinical psychologist, couples therapist, and relationship researcher, I have grown increasingly alarmed and frustrated by where we are and where we seem to be going. I attend conferences that are led by "gurus" who preach new and shiny ideas about how we work through and resolve issues in coupledom—yet none are rooted in science and biology. For the past forty-plus years, I've been in search of empirical evidence regarding the way we form attachments, what makes us feel secure, and how to bridge the gap of couples' varying attachment needs and fears. I have always believed that love is exquisitely logical and understandable, adaptive and functional. Even better, it is malleable, reparable, and durable. This belief in the science of love was what inspired me to create Emotionally Focused Therapy— EFT—which is at the center of my 2008 book, *Hold Me Tight: Seven Conversations for a Lifetime of Love.*

I realize that for couples in distressed love relationships, science is the last thing on their minds. It is not the path they think to take to return to their healthy state of secure attachment and bonding with one another. But to echo a popular recent catchphrase, we need to believe the science.

Consider the brain scan study done with psychologist Jim Coan from the University of Virginia: Women patients having an fMRI brain scan were told that when a little red light in the machine came on, they might receive a small electric shock—or they might not. As they anticipated this potential shock, their partners were prompted to hold their hands and speak words of compassion and love to them. Coan found that encouraging words and touch from a loved one completely changed how their brain responded to the threat of shock—and to the shock itself. Patients registered less stress and felt less pain.

Based on what this experiment and hundreds of other studies like it show, being bonded with a loved one acts as a buffer to pain and distress. So it is precisely this time in our history when romantic love should be more important than ever. The aftermath of the pandemic has led to an epidemic of loneliness, anxiety, and depression. Today, adult partnerships are often the only real human ties we can count on in our virtual and frenetically multitasking world. Moreover, we seem, in so many ways, to be working actively against our desire for love and commitment. Our society exalts emotional independence, and we're constantly exhorted to love ourselves first and foremost. It's a growing trend that worries me, and in the past few years, I've felt the call to offer couples an additional resource that can help them rediscover one another and strengthen their bond.

I also have become even more firm in my belief in EFT's universality, and how the research on its effectiveness proves that we are more alike than different. Over the decades, I've seen firsthand how EFT has helped couples, no matter their race, ethnicity, faith, sexual orientation, gender identity, or political affiliation. I've heard from couples all around the world, from a tapestry of experiences and worldviews: from Muslim couples in Egypt to Evangelicals in the Southern U.S.; white, Black, cisgender, and queer. Whatever our differences, it's clear that every human being is wired for connection—we all share common needs to be seen, valued, and supported by others. Now more than ever, that's a truth we need to be reminded of.

WHY A WORKBOOK? WHY NOW?

Context, practice, process. These are the ways we learn, teach, grow, and expand ourselves. Without these things, we just hear words, lectures are just moments of preachiness, and facts without stories are fast forgotten. In *Hold Me Tight* and my subsequent book *Love Sense,* I offered my lifetime of research, principles, and findings, along with case studies of dozens of couples who have benefited from EFT in their relationships. I combined and analyzed the clinical studies, laboratory experiments, and applied therapies of my own and of other scientists who have proven that love is our basic survival code—an essential task of our mammalian brain that compels us to read and respond to others. But just as a physical therapist would need to touch and prod your aching body to find out the source of your pain, EFT can only heal a distressed couple when their relationship can be touched and manipulated, tested and experienced. This workbook is based on my book *Hold Me Tight: Seven Conversations for a Lifetime of Love,* which has been translated into twenty-four languages and has sold more than one million copies. I also developed the Hold Me Tight® Relationship Education tion Program based on the book, which has also been translated into a variety of languages and is facilitated in many countries across countless cultures. Having been adapted for specific groups such as Christian couples, families with teens and with adult children, and couples facing cardiac disease, the program is also now available in an online format. This workbook takes the Hold Me Tight® theories and shows you how to apply them to *your* specific relationship, to use on an everyday basis. You provide the context and I'll lead you through the practice and process.

WHAT TO EXPECT FROM EFT AND THIS WORKBOOK

Love relationships are not bargains; they are emotional bonds based on our innate need for safe and emotional connection. You can't bargain for compassion, for connection. These are not intellectual reactions; they are *emotional* responses. Emotionally Focused Therapy teaches couples to recognize their emotional rhythms and patterns in the dance of romantic love. Before we enter romantic relationships, this biological need for emotional attachment was satisfied (appropriately or not) by our parents. EFT is based on the notion that the attachment bond happens between adults, too. This was a breakthrough when it came to understanding partners' roles in their love relationships, and subsequently, their roles in the breakdown of the trust that is meant to bond them.

So forget what other therapies say to do, such as learning how to argue better, analyzing your childhood, making grand romantic gestures, or experimenting with new sexual positions. Instead, recognize and admit that you are emotionally attached to and dependent on your partner in much the same way that a child is dependent on a parent for nurturing, soothing, and protection. Partners need to pinpoint and share their vulnerabilities and needs in positive ways that lead to bonding moments. This is especially true given that your partner *will* trigger these vulnerabilities — we are all so fearful of rejection and abandonment. A successful couple must learn how to deal with these sensitivities in ways that build trust and intimacy.

EFT and the exercises in this workbook focus on creating and strengthening the emotional bond between partners by identifying and transforming the key moments that foster a loving adult relationship: being open, attuned, and responsive to one another.

This workbook is for *all* couples—*all* partners seeking a lifetime of love in a partnership of their design. It is for people from all walks of life, of all lifestyles, because everyone on this planet has the same longing for connection.

Through exercises and discussions based on the seven conversations featured in *Hold Me Tight,* you will capture the defining moments in your love relationship and learn how to shape these moments to create a secure and lasting bond. *Hold Me Tight* is not required reading to be able to use this workbook. If you have read the book, you will find this additional material fortifying and the exercises novel. If you are diving right into the workbook without having read the book, rest assured that the exercises are supported by some foundational material and will be self-explanatory and fulfilling to complete.

THE GOALS AS YOU MOVE THROUGH THIS WORKBOOK ARE TO:

- Better understand romantic love—the pivotal moves and moments that define a relationship and can either lead to the mountaintop or take you down the rabbit hole.
- Better understand your partner's and your own emotional responses and needs.
- Be able to describe and control negative interactions and spirals that create pain and distance.
- Be able to shape positive moments of reaching and responding that create a secure bond.

While the success of EFT is enjoyed by couples practicing it together, it's important to understand attachment on an individual personal level, which is why you'll find some exercises designed to be done alone, some introspective, others meditative. You'll find true or false and fill-in-the-blank worksheets, journal prompts, checklists, and sample dialogues to help bring your EFT experience to life. Relax with it and have fun. There are no right or wrong answers.

SOME PRACTICAL SUGGESTIONS ON HOW TO USE THIS WORKBOOK

You can choose to engage in the conversations in different ways. For example, you may want to do one conversation per day, one per week, or designate a weekend when you will be able to break from the day-to-day and commit to your introspection and to one another. I don't recommend cramming. One per week will give you an opportunity to get acquainted with the goals of each conversation and the methods within them, and to check in with yourself and one another without feeling pressured to move on. You may even feel that you need to spend some more time on a particular conversation.

The conversations are designed to be done in succession, so I do not recommend jumping around. However, you may want to alter the sequence or skip a conversation if you both do not think it's relevant to your relationship.

The preferred way to do the work is to do it together and share answers with one another. There may be times, however, when you wish to do some exercise by yourself. That is okay, too. As stated already, some exercises are purposely solo projects. You may want to photocopy or scan any pages that you want to do by yourself and place them in a binder for safekeeping.

For couples who are comfortable sharing, you may want to fill in the exercises using different colored pencils or alternate who answers first. You will find a rhythm that works for you. This should not be a tense experience. Consider it a journey of discovering yourself (perhaps for the first time) and rediscovering your relationship.

I know it can be hard to *begin* the work of love and loving. But what I know is this: The work is well worth it. Our need for others to come close when we call—to offer us safe haven—is absolute, but not absolutely given. We must work at it, and you have already begun by simply picking up this workbook and discussing together the role it can play in your relationship. It may not lead to a perfect love (because there is no such thing), but it will lead to a more present love—one that is secure, deep, and lasting.

Our Emotional Responses and the Language of Attachment

Love may be the most used and the most potent word in every language spoken around the world. It is the pinnacle of evolution, the most compelling survival mechanism of the human species. Not because it induces us to mate and reproduce, but because love drives us to bond emotionally with a precious few others who offer us refuge from the storms of life. Love is our bulwark, designed to provide emotional protection so we can cope with the ups and downs of existence.

This is the drive to emotionally attach—to find someone to whom we can say, "Hold me tight." Emotional connection, a felt sense of closeness, is biologically coded as a safety cue in our genes, brains, and bodies. It is as basic to life, health, and happiness as the drives for food, shelter, or sex. We need emotional attachments with a few irreplaceable others to be physically and mentally healthy—to survive. Secure connection to a loved one is empowering. It anchors us in feelings of safety and security. Science from all fields tells us very clearly that we are not only social animals, but animals who need a special kind of close connection with others. It's not just whether or not we have close relationships in our lives—the quality of these relationships matters, too. Negative relationships undermine our health. When we are disconnected emotionally from our partners, we don't feel emotionally safe. In a secure bond, we are accessible and responsive. Secure attachment and bonding make us feel safe, while insecure attachment makes us afraid. Just as connection and protection act as signals that tell us we are safe, isolation and emotional separation from our partners are danger cues.

We all experience fear when we have disagreements or arguments with our partner. But for those of us with secure bonds, it is a momentary blip. The fear is quickly and easily tamped down as we realize that there is no real threat or that our partner will reassure us if we ask. For those of us with weaker or fraying bonds, the fear can be overwhelming. We are swamped by what neuroscientist Jaak Panksepp calls *primal panic*. Then we generally do one of two things: We either become *demanding* and clingy in an effort to draw comfort and reassurance from our partner, or we *withdraw* and detach in an attempt to soothe and protect ourselves. No matter the exact words, what we're really saying in those reactions is, "Notice me. Be with me. I need you," or "I won't let you hurt me. I will chill out, try to stay in control."

The exercises in this section will help you discover not just your level of fear of losing trust and attachment, that safe and emotional connection we are wired to seek, but also the manner in which you act out in the face of what you feel is threatening your bond. This is an important step to undergo before the conversations begin, because before you can communicate effectively with your partner and your partner with you, it is necessary to find clarity within oneself regarding your own attachment language in the form of your needs, patterns, and behaviors. Only then can accountability come into play, a key driver to hearing and answering with compassion one another's calls for attention and connection. When you know how to speak the language of attachment, you can give clear messages about what you need and how much you care.

DEMAND AND WITHDRAW: IDENTIFYING YOUR PRIMAL PANIC

Attachment theory teaches us that our loved one is our shelter in life. When that person is emotionally unavailable or unresponsive, we face being out in the cold, alone and helpless. We are assailed by emotions—anger, sadness, hurt, and, above all, fear. This is not surprising when we remember that fear is our built-in alarm system; the bells go off when our survival is threatened. Losing connection with our loved one jeopardizes our sense of security, triggering the amygdala, the part of the brain that senses fear. We don't think; we feel, we act. At this point, two responses typically occur: We *demand* or we *withdraw.*

The strategies for dealing with the fear of losing connection are unconscious, and they might work, at least in the beginning. But as distressed partners resort to them more and more, they set up vicious spirals of insecurity that only push them further and further apart. More and more interactions occur in which neither partner feels safe, both become defensive, and each is left assuming the very worst about one another and their relationship. It's a dance, a delicate one, in which we step together in sync or step on one another's toes in a choreography of panic and fear. How we each emotionally respond—demand, withdraw, or any combination of the two—indicates to us how beautiful (or not) our dance is.

Before we can name the dance you are in together, see if you can identify your individual steps using this introspective journal exercise.

LET'S GET INTROSPECTIVE:
Journal Exercise

Our fears are wired into our brains. Everyone has them. Can you pinpoint or identify your fears? Listen to the feelings you have, and find, at the core, any fear or anxiety that involves being rejected or abandoned by your partner. To help you get in touch with your internal experience, here are a few of the common feelings or qualities of demanders and withdrawers. Check off the ones you resonate with.

DEMANDERS OFTEN FEEL:

☐ Frightened of their aloneness; scared they're not wanted

☐ Afraid of being abandoned

☐ Frightened of their feelings of hurt

☐ Scared of being invisible

WITHDRAWERS OFTEN FEEL:

☐ Frightened of rejection

☐ Scared of their experience of disappointing their partner—coming up short

☐ Afraid of failure

☐ Overwhelmed

☐ Numbed or frozen with fear

☐ Afraid of being judged or criticized

Reflect on what scares you most.

PARTNER 1:

....

....

....

....

PARTNER 2:

....

....

....

....

CHECKPOINT: What Your Words Might Mean

Demanders say:

I'm dying here. I am shut down. My feelings don't matter. It's lonelier than living alone. By myself. Dismissed. I get no response. I'm hammering on their door. I yell to get a response—any response. We're roommates. I don't matter to them.

Withdrawers say:

I never get it right—can't please. I give up, space out. Best to avoid a fight—try to keep things calm. I'm failing here. Paralyzed. No point. Go behind my wall. I try to *fix* it—but it doesn't work. I numb out.

A.R.E.: ACCESSIBILITY, RESPONSIVENESS, AND ENGAGEMENT

The key question in our love relationships is, "Are you there for me?" This translates to, "Do I matter to you? Can I reach you? Are you accessible, emotionally available to me? Can I rely on you to respond when I need you? Will you engage with me, give me your attention?"

"Are you there for me?" is the A.R.E. question. This key question is buried, hidden just under the surface in most recurring arguments about pragmatic issues such as chores, personality differences, sex, children, and money. If partners feel safe and loved, they can deal with differences and problems together. If not, then relationship issues and fears get channeled into endless disagreements.

QUESTIONNAIRE: How A.R.E. You?

Does your partner's perception of how accessible, responsive, and emotionally engaged you are, fit with your view of yourself and how safe your relationship is? Read each statement and circle T for *true* or F for *false*. You can complete the questionnaire individually, then either reflect on the answers on your own, or discuss your answers together.

From your viewpoint, is your partner available to you?

1. I can get my partner's attention easily.   T   F

2. My partner is easy to connect with   T   F
    emotionally.

3. My partner shows me that I come first   T   F
    with them.

4. I am not feeling lonely or shut out in this   T   F
    relationship.

5. I can share my deepest feelings with my   T   F
    partner. They will listen.

From your viewpoint, is your partner responsive to you?

1. If I need connection and comfort, they   T   F
    will be there for me.

2. My partner responds to signals that   T   F
    I need them to come close.

3. I find I can lean on my partner when I am   T   F
    anxious or unsure.

4. Even when we fight or disagree, I know   T   F
    that I am important to my partner and we
    will find a way to come together.

5. If I need reassurance about how important   T   F
    I am to my partner, I can get it.

Are you positively emotionally engaged with one another?

1. I feel comfortable being close to and trusting   T   F
    my partner.

2. I can confide in my partner about almost   T   F
    anything.

3. I feel confident, even when we are apart,   T   F
    that we're connected to one another.

4. I know that my partner cares about my   T   F
    joys, hurts, and fears.

5. I feel safe enough to take emotional risks   T   F
    with my partner.

UNDERSTANDING YOUR
PRIMAL PANIC RESPONSE

See if you can plot out the steps in the usual negative dance that you find yourself caught in with your partner. When you suddenly find that you do not feel safely connected to your partner, what do you usually do? See if you can find descriptors in the lists below that fit for you. Check off as many as you resonate with. Share this with your partner.

WHEN I DON'T FEEL SAFELY CONNECTED TO YOU, I OFTEN
DEMAND BY:

- ☐ Complaining
- ☐ Becoming critical
- ☐ Blaming or pointing out your mistakes
- ☐ Yelling
- ☐ Telling you how to improve
- ☐ Becoming angry—blowing up
- ☐ Insisting on making my point even if I get pushy
- ☐ Expressing frustration in an angry way
- ☐ Expressing disapproval
- ☐ Defining you as being *the* problem
- ☐ Pursuing—insisting that you pay attention
- ☐ Telling you how to change
- ☐ Making threats
- ☐ Prodding

I MOVE AWAY FROM YOU (*WITHDRAW*) BY:

☐ Trying to zone out

☐ Staying calm and reasoning with you

☐ Shutting you out

☐ Stopping the conversation by leaving or turning to a task

☐ Not listening and numbing out

☐ Changing the subject

☐ Defending myself and showing you that you are wrong

☐ Finding an exit—just trying to get away

☐ Staying in my head and just not responding

☐ Going into my shell like a turtle

☐ Protecting myself by distancing

☐ Refusing to talk and leaving

☐ Giving up

Our actions have more impact on our partners than we think. How do you think your partner sees you in these moments? For instance, if you often get angry and demanding, you might think your partner would describe you as scary? Or, if you are continually telling them that they are inadequate as a partner and a person, pushing them away, rejecting them and the relationship, then you might be seen by your partner as abandoning them, as not needing them, as being easily able to shut them out as if they don't matter, leaving them painfully alone.

LET'S GET INTROSPECTIVE:
Journal Exercise

Consider what attracted you to your partner and what you like about them.

PARTNER 1:

....

....

....

....

PARTNER 2:

....

....

....

....

My partner might see me as:

PARTNER 1:

....

....

....

....

....

PARTNER 2:

....

....

....

....

....

See if you can agree on your main response. Do you mainly demand or withdraw?

PARTNER 1:

....

....

....

....

....

PARTNER 2:

....

....

....

....

....

Do you and your partner have different or similar primal panic responses? It's important to identify yours and then compare to your partner's, as this helps identify the kind of dance you are in.

PARTNER 1:

....

....

....

....

PARTNER 2:

....

....

....

....

We will further explore and dissect this in the next chapter with exercises that are all about the three different types of dances that couples take part in, depending on their primal panic responses. But first, let's map your individual moves using the following worksheet.

WORKSHEET: Mapping Your Moves

Fill in the cue that starts up the music of disconnection. Try to avoid making general or abstract statements that could be disguises for blaming. Examples could include when one partner says to another, "Well, you are just being difficult, as usual," or "There you go getting emotional again." Try to be concrete and specific, as big sweeping general comments are overwhelming and trigger alarms in a person's fight-or-flight response. Once we are in alarm mode, our ability to listen and respond to information diminishes. So instead of saying a partner is "difficult," one could say, "Right now you seem so far away—you're not listening to me."

Example responses include:

...you say you are too tired for sex and we have not made love for a few weeks.

...we fight about my child-rearing or parenting style.

...we don't seem to speak for days.

Partner 1:

When _____

_____,

I do not feel safely connected to you.

Partner 2:

When _____

_____,

I do not feel safely connected to you.

Partner 1:

1. **For the following statement, choose a verb, e.g.,**
   complain, nag, zone out, ignore you, run, move away.

   I tend to _____.

   I move this way to try to cope with difficult feelings and find a way to change our dance.

2. **State the hope that pulls you into the dance, e.g.,**
   We will avoid more conflict, **or** *I will persuade you to respond more to me.*

   I do it in the hope that _____

   _____.

3. **Identify a feeling. The usual ones people identify at this point are** *frustrated, angry, numb, empty,* **or** *confused.*

   As this pattern keeps going, I feel _____

   _____.

4. **Summarize the most catastrophic conclusion you can imagine, e.g., *You do not care about us, I am not important to you,* or *I can never please you.***

   What I then say to myself about our relationship is _____

   _____

   _____.

5. **Choose a phrase that best describes the action of your partner, e.g., *shut down, push me to respond.***

   My understanding of the circular dance that makes it harder and harder for us to safely connect is that when I move in the way I described above, you seem to then

   _____

   _____.

6. **Insert verbs that describe your and your partner's moves in the dance, e.g., *The more I hide out, the more you harp on me to be heard.***

   The more I _____,

   the more you _____.

   We are then both trapped in pain and isolation.

Partner 2:

1. **For the following statement, choose a verb, e.g.,** *complain, nag, zone out, ignore you, run, move away.*

   I tend to _____.
   I move this way to try to cope with difficult feelings and find a way to change our dance.

2. **State the hope that pulls you into the dance, e.g.,** *We will avoid more conflict,* **or** *I will persuade you to respond more to me.*

   I do it in the hope that _____
   _____.

3. **Identify a feeling. The usual ones people identify at this point are** *frustrated, angry, numb, empty,* **or** *confused.*

   As this pattern keeps going, I feel _____
   _____.

4. **Summarize the most catastrophic conclusion you can imagine, e.g.,** *You do not care about us, I am not important to you,* **or** *I can never please you.*

What I then say to myself about our relationship is _____

_____

_____.

5. **Choose a phrase that best describes the action of your partner, e.g.,** *shut down, push me to respond.*

My understanding of the circular dance that makes it harder and harder for us to safely connect is that when I move in the way I described above, you seem to then

_____

_____.

6. **Insert verbs that describe your and your partner's moves in the dance, e.g.,** *The more I hide out, the more you harp on me to be heard.*

The more I _____,

the more you _____.

We are then both trapped in pain and isolation.

Once you can identify these negative cycles and recognize that they trap you both, give a name to the kind of dance you are in. I've had couples call their dance the Spiral, the Tornado, and the Black Hole. Whatever you call it, this is your Demon Dialogue.

30

Our Demon Dialogue

....

....

While it's encouraged for couples to name their own Demon Dialogue, I have identified three over the last several decades that you can explore in the next chapter.

Hold These Tight

- Emotional responsiveness is the key to love.
- Fear is at the heart of our panic responses.
- The demand–withdraw pattern happens when our connection is out of step.
- A safe, loving, lasting relationship is entirely possible if we learn to dance together.

....

Recognizing the Demon Dialogues

You have just explored your attachment needs and panic responses, and those of your partner. When we do not understand love and our attachment needs, we remain blind to the impact that our primal panic responses have on our partner and vice versa. If we cannot reach and connect, we try secondary strategies. We either try to turn off our attachment feelings and needs and withdraw (we turn away from our partner), or we turn up our feelings and demand or criticize our partner (we turn against them to gain a sense of control). Through countless sessions with couples, I have seen how this out-of-step dance plays out during intense conversations. You might recall from *Hold Me Tight* that the demand–withdraw dance typically results in three different dialogues, which I call Demon Dialogues.

DEMON DIALOGUE 1:
FIND THE BAD GUY

Let's face it: Most of us are good at blaming. "It's not my fault; the other one is the bad guy." This dialogue could easily be called It's Not Me, It's You. Here we concentrate on each step and *how* "you just stepped on me," instead of assessing the whole dance. Mark each of the following statements as *Agree* or *Disagree* to determine whether Find the Bad Guy is your Demon Dialogue.

1. I find myself expecting negativity and blame, even watching for it and reacting to it faster when I think I see it coming.   **Agree**   **Disagree**

2. I cannot relax with my partner, and certainly cannot connect with or confide in them.   **Agree**   **Disagree**

3. I can't stop thinking it is my partner who is mostly to blame.   **Agree**   **Disagree**

4. I have a laundry list of past complaints that I use when I feel my partner is criticizing me.   **Agree**   **Disagree**

5. I don't feel satisfied unless I get a jab in to exert power, letting my partner know I can't be hurt.   **Agree**   **Disagree**

6. I want to force my partner to hear me, and   **Agree**   **Disagree**
   I'll go to great lengths to keep on a subject,
   no matter what.

7. I want my partner to take me into account.   **Agree**   **Disagree**

CHECKPOINT

Find the Bad Guy fights tend to…

   …define the other person/relationship in absolutes, using words like "always" and "never," along with labels that blame, e.g., "You are always so unreasonable—so immature."

   …include anger and rage as the dominant emotions.

   …see both partners trapped in "attack-attack" mode.

The dance goes like this:

   The more you attack…

   …the more dangerous you appear.

   …the more I watch my back.

   …the harder I hit back.

   …and then, the more you attack in return.

   The dance goes on.

LET'S GET INTROSPECTIVE:
Journal Exercise

When a couple's pattern is attack-attack, each one sets out to win at all costs. These questions and reflections can help you think about how you and your partner move in this dialogue when both of you get caught in fight-to-win mode.

Reflect on the last incident between you and your partner. Maybe you were late home from work and forgot to call, or your child acted in the least expected way, which upset you, or maybe one of you left a mess or broke a sentimental item. How did you accuse your partner? What did you use to win the fight and prove your innocence? What are your usual comebacks when you feel cornered?

PARTNER 1:

....

....

....

....

....

PARTNER 2:

....

....

....

....

....

Sketch out the circle of hostile criticism and labeling that trapped you both. How did each of you begin to define the other? How did each of you wind up and enrage the other? Was there a winner? (Probably not.)

PARTNER 1:

....

....

....

....

....

PARTNER 2:

....

....

....

....

....

What happened after your Find the Bad Guy fight? For instance, "We iced one another out for two days. One partner took a dive into hopelessness and depression, and we both felt so alone and hopeless."

PARTNER 1:

....

....

....

....

....

PARTNER 2:

....

....

....

....

....

How did you feel about yourself, your partner, the connection between you?

PARTNER 1:

....

....

....

....

PARTNER 2:

....

....

....

....

....

Were you able to go back and talk about the fight and console one another? If not, how did you deal with the loss of safety between you?

PARTNER 1:

....

....

....

....

PARTNER 2:

_____

_____

_____

_____

_____

Next time you find yourselves in fight-to-win mode, engage in the following corrective dialogue:

"We are starting to label one another to prove the other one is the bad guy. We are just going to get hurt more if we get stuck in this dance. Let's not get caught in an attack-attack dance with one another. Maybe we can talk about what happened without it being anyone's fault."

DEMON DIALOGUE 2:
THE PROTEST POLKA

This is the most common and ensnaring dance in relationships. The Protest Polka creates a loop, each move calling forth and reinforcing the next. One partner reaches out, albeit in a negative way (demand), and the other steps back (withdraw), and the pattern repeats. The dance goes on forever because the emotions and needs behind the dance are the most powerful on this planet. Attachment relationships are the only ties on Earth where *any* response is better than none. When we get no emotional response from a loved one, we are wired to protest. The Protest Polka is all about trying to get a response that connects and reassures.

CHECKPOINT

The Protest Polka is:

   The dominant, most often occurring dance of distress.

   Deadly to love relationships.

   All about attachment—both partners are protesting disconnection.

   Ambiguous messages, such as, "Well, maybe I don't want to be here, so…" or "Perhaps I am just not enough for you, so then…" or "I should just give up and…"

   An endless dance, driven by a primal survival code of attachment, and fueled by high-octane emotions.

The dance goes like this:

The more disconnected/dismissed I feel…

…the more I complain.

…the more I demand.

…the more I get critical.

…the more I pursue you.

The more dangerous I appear…

…the more you move away.

…the more you defend.

…the more you shut down and shut me out.

LET'S GET INTROSPECTIVE:
Journal Exercise

Do you agree with any or all of the following statements that characterize those who demand when their secure bond feels threatened? Put a check mark next to the ones that feel familiar.

☐ I have a broken heart. I could weep forever. Sometimes I feel like I'm dying in this relationship.

☐ These days my partner is always busy, somewhere else. Even when at home, they're on the computer or watching TV. We seem to live on separate planets. I am shut out.

☐ Sometimes I think that I am lonelier in this relationship than I was when I lived by myself. It seemed easier to be by myself than to live like this—together but separate.

☐ I needed my partner so much during that time and they were just so distant. My feelings didn't seem to matter. My partner just dismissed them.

☐ We are roommates. We never seem to be close anymore.

☐ I get mad, sure I do. My partner just doesn't seem to care, so I sometimes lash out. I'm just trying to get a response, any response.

☐ I am just not sure I matter to my partner. It's like I'm not being seen. I don't know how to reach them.

☐ If I didn't push and push, we would never be close. It would never happen.

Do you agree with any of the following statements that characterize those who withdraw when their secure bond feels threatened? Put a check mark next to the ones that feel familiar.

☐ I can never get it right with my partner, so I just give up. It all seems hopeless.

☐ I feel numb. Don't know how I feel. So I just freeze up and space out.

☐ I get that I am flawed somehow. I am a failure as a partner. Somehow that truth just paralyzes me.

☐ I shut down and wait for my partner to calm down. I try to keep everything calm, not rock the boat. That is my way of taking care of the relationship. Don't rock the boat.

☐ I go into my shell where it's safe. I go behind my wall. I try to shut the door on all my partner's angry comments. I am the prisoner and my partner's the judge.

☐ I feel like nothing in this relationship. Inadequate. So I run to my computer, job, or hobbies. At work, I am somebody. I don't think I am anything special to my partner at all.

☐ I don't matter to my partner. I am way down on the list. I come somewhere after the kids, the house, and friends. Hell, even the dog comes before me! I just help pay the bills. So I end up feeling empty. You never know if the love will be there.

☐ I don't feel that I need anyone the way my partner does. I am just not as needy. I was always taught that it's weak to let yourself need someone like that, childish. So I try to handle things on my own. I just walk away.

☐ I don't know what my partner is talking about. We are fine. This is what marriage is all about. You just become friends. I am not sure I know what is meant by *close,* anyway.

☐ I try to solve the problem in concrete ways. Try to fix it. I deal with it in my head. It doesn't work. My partner doesn't want that. I don't know what my partner wants.

WORKSHEET: Feeling Out the Feedback Loop

If you feel comfortable, see if you can pin down each person's moves in the Protest Polka. Can you see the feedback loop? Describe it very simply by filling in the blanks in the following sentences. For example:

Partner 1: The more I ***question where you've been,*** the more you ***are snarky and cold*** and then the more I ***accuse you,*** and round and round we go.

Partner 2: The more I ***reply with sarcasm,*** the more you ***yell*** and then the more I ***walk away,*** and round and round we go.

Now you try it:

Partner 1: The more I _____,

the more you _____

and then the more I _____,

and round and round we go.

Partner 2: The more I _____,

the more you _____

and then the more I _____,

and round and round we go.

CHECKPOINT: Mantras Make a Difference

The Protest Polka becomes a vicious cycle that spirals couples to an almost certain breaking point. Research has shown that couples who do not learn to recognize this pattern and change the music typically do not stay together past their fifth year. Breaking the cycle requires five things — things I've learned from watching partners work together over the years. There are vows you can make to yourself (and one another) in the form of mantras when you see the Demon Dialogue taking hold.

1. **You have to see it. The whole enchilada. You have to see the *how* of the dance between you and your partner.**

   Mantra: We will not focus on specific steps, especially the other person's. There is no more, "You just attacked me." We will step back and see the entire picture.

2. **You must both grasp how the moves of each partner pull the other into the dance. Each of you is trapped in the dance and unwittingly helps to trap the other.**

   Mantra: I will take note of how you are responding to my attack or withdrawal. I will stop to notice the ripple effects that my actions and behavior have on you.

3. **The Protest Polka is all about attachment distress. It cannot be stopped with logical problem-solving or formal communication. You have to know the nature of**

the dance if you are to change the key elements and return to safe connection.

Mantra: We will learn to recognize calls for connection and how desperation turns into "I push, I poke, anything for a response." We will remember these patterns are universal because our needs and fears, and our responses to perceived loss and separation, are universal.

4. **You need to understand the nature of love, and tune in to these moments of disconnection and the protest and distress that are the key part of the Protest Polka.**

Mantra: We can learn to see the Protest Polka as the enemy, not our partner.

5. **You must begin to stand together and call the enemy by name, so you can slow down the music.**

Mantra: We can step to the side and create enough safety to talk about attachment emotions and needs.

DEMON DIALOGUE 3: FREEZE AND FLEE

Sometimes, when a couple comes to see me, I do not hear the hostility of Find the Bad Guy or the frantic beat of the Protest Polka. I hear a deadly silence. If we think of a relationship as a dance, then here both partners are sitting it out! It looks like there is nothing at stake; no one seems to be invested in the dance. Except that there is a palpable tension in the air and pain is clear on the couple's faces. Emotion theorists tell us that we can try to suppress our emotions but it just doesn't work. In Freeze and Flee, both partners are shut down into frozen defense and denial. Each is in self-protection mode, trying to act as if they do not feel and do not need one another.

CHECKPOINT

Freeze and Flee is all about:

Mutual withdrawal. Frozen defense and denial. Neither partner is risking reaching out to the other.

Hopelessness. No sex, no touch. Partners are strangers to one another. Often the aftermath of chronic Protest Polka.

Icy emptiness. Prelude to detachment.

The dance goes like this:

The more I hold back and shut down my feelings, the more careful and distant you become.

The extreme distancing of Freeze and Flee is a response to the loss of connection and the sense of helplessness about how to restore it. The real problem with the Freeze and Flee pattern is the hopelessness that colors it. Both partners decide that their difficulty lies in themselves, in their innate flaws. Shame takes over and people decide there must be something wrong with them or that they are just unlovable. The natural response to this is to hide, to conceal one's unlovable self.

Many couples I've worked with who are stuck in the Freeze and Flee pattern deny their needs for emotional closeness and withdraw when they each feel disconnected. Our history with loved ones shapes our present relationships. In moments of disconnection when we cannot safely engage with our lover, we naturally turn to the way of coping that we adopted as a child, the way of coping that allowed us to hold on to our parents, at least in some minimal way. When we feel the hot emotions that warn us our connection is in trouble, as you explored in the first chapter of this workbook, we automatically try to shut them down and flee into reason and distracting activities. In this dance of distance, avoiding these emotions becomes an end in itself.

QUESTIONNAIRE: Do I Freeze and Flee?

Circle Often, Sometimes, or Never for each of the following statements:

My avoidance just happens without me choosing the response; it's automatic, I don't even think about it.	**Often**	**Sometimes**	**Never**
I look back and believe my upbringing was cold and distant.	**Often**	**Sometimes**	**Never**
I don't want to feel rejection, so I build up a wall, not only in my relationship but in many areas of my life where I feel vulnerable.	**Often**	**Sometimes**	**Never**
I make a hobby out of beating myself up, secretly ashamed of the failure I am in my relationships.	**Often**	**Sometimes**	**Never**
I seek out attention from anybody who is not my partner, including my children and pets.	**Often**	**Sometimes**	**Never**
I think my partner deserves much better than I can offer.	**Often**	**Sometimes**	**Never**

LET'S GET INTROSPECTIVE:
Journal Exercise

Does the Freeze and Flee pattern seem familiar to you? If so, where did you learn to ignore and discount your need for emotional connection? Who taught you to do this? When do you feel most alone?

PARTNER 1:

....

....

....

....

....

....

PARTNER 2:

....

....

....

....

....

....

....

Can you dare to share your answers to these questions with your partner? Can you share the one cue that sparks the distancing dance? It can be as simple as a turn of the head at a particular moment or not being looked at when you are speaking.

PARTNER 1:

....

....

....

....

....

....

....

PARTNER 2:

....

....

....

....

....

....

....

Can you identify exactly how you push your partner away from you or make it dangerous for them to come closer?

PARTNER 1:

....

....

....

PARTNER 2:

What do you tell yourself once you have emotionally withdrawn to justify separation and to discourage yourself from reaching out to your partner? Sometimes these pronouncements signal what you think love is and how you think you ought to act in love relationships, often formed by what you might have learned as a child from your parents or even cues from a particular culture. For example, some are taught rules like, "If you can't say anything nice then don't say anything at all," or, "Men just cannot be responsive or intimate." Can you share these with your partner?

PARTNER 1:

....

....

....

....

....

....

....

PARTNER 2:

_____

_____

_____

_____

_____

_____

_____

On the next page, make a list of all the things this dance has taken away from you as a couple. Maybe you are losing your faith that you can count on this relationship; perhaps your sense of being special to one another has diminished, or your ability to play and have fun. Perhaps you're not getting those special hugs anymore. We usually have glimpses of emotional closeness when we first become infatuated with a person and are willing to take any risk to be with them. We can remember these moments, just as we remember our hopes and longings. Reflect on how this negative dance may have eroded these things.

Our List of Things Lost

....

....

....

....

....

....

Hold These Tight
....

FIND THE BAD GUY

Purpose: Self-protection
- Attack-attack pattern
- Both partners are accusing and blaming.

PROTEST POLKA

Purpose: To get a response that connects and reassures
- One partner is demanding, actively protesting the disconnection; the other is withdrawing, quietly protesting the implied criticism.
- Each partner is missing the other's signals.

FREEZE AND FLEE

Purpose: Frozen self- defense, and denial

- Frequently evolves from the Protest Polka, after the pursuing, critical (demanding) partner gives up trying to get their partner's attention and goes silent.
- No emotional connection.

Finding the Raw Spots

We all have raw spots. I define them as a hypersensitivity, formed by moments in a person's past or current relationships when an attachment need has been repeatedly neglected, ignored, or dismissed, resulting in feeling what I call the *2 Ds*—emotionally *deprived* or *deserted*. The 2 Ds are universal raw spots for lovers.

These sensitivities frequently arise from wounded relationships with significant people in our past, especially parents, who give us our basic template for loving relationships, siblings and other members of our families, and, of course, past and present lovers. For example, when my husband's eyelids began drooping while I was speaking to him, I hit the ceiling, enraged. He was tired and drowsy, but it sent me back to days when an ex-partner would fall instantly asleep every time I tried to start a serious conversation. Dozing off was a not-so-subtle form of withdrawing, disconnecting from the relationship. This experience made me hypervigilant—sudden sleepiness signals emotional abandonment (my raw spot) for me.

We do not choose to have these vulnerabilities. Our brains respond to signals from our partner in terms of safety and danger because connection with special others is so key to our survival; the instinct to survive explains why these fears are like a low-grade punch in the gut. Being vulnerable comes with the territory in love relationships. The choice is in how we deal with these vulnerabilities.

If you find yourself continually stuck in a Demon Dialogue with your partner, you can bet it is being sparked by attempts to deal with the pain of a raw spot, or more likely, raw spots in both of you. Unfortunately, your raw spots almost inevitably rub against one another's. Chafe one in your partner and their reaction might often irritate one in you.

The more securely attached a couple is, the more they can be open about these vulnerabilities and help one another with them. They learn to soothe one another in their sore places. Each time they do so, the relationship becomes safer and trust deepens. If they cannot do this, then when these raw spots are touched, partners are more likely to get angry or shut down and get caught in the Demon Dialogues. These interactions then make raw spots more and more painful, and keep the Demon Dialogues going indefinitely.

CHECK ANY OF THE FOLLOWING UNIVERSAL RAW SPOTS
THAT SEEM FAMILIAR TO YOU:

☐ Feeling deprived of comforting contact
☐ Feeling a lack of attention and safe connection

☐ Feeling deserted when your partner does not respond to your need for closeness

☐ Feeling rejected when you get messages that you are disappointing and not wanted

Raw spots can surface because of past wounds, even in generally happy relationships. Raw spots mark our vulnerable places—places where we have been wounded before. They represent the fears that are easily triggered. When a raw spot is rubbed, it sends a danger signal and fear immediately overwhelms and floods us. Raw spots can occur during big transitions or crises—for instance, when becoming a parent, becoming ill, or losing a job. Maybe when you were younger and you asked for reassurance of your mother's love, she said you were "being silly." It's more than likely that to be called silly now that you're an adult causes you to spiral into the same insecure feeling you had as a child. Raw spots can also develop when a partner seems chronically indifferent, producing an overwhelming sense of hurt that then infuses even small issues. The failure of our loved one to respond scrapes our emotional skin raw.

SURFACE VERSUS SOFTER FEELINGS: CONTROLLING THE NARRATIVE

Emotion is *fast*. It moves us in a nanosecond. We have to slow down to even recognize the softer feelings such as hurt or fear underneath our reactions of anger or defensiveness or withdrawal. When a raw spot is hit, you suddenly find yourself off-balance and disorganized. Your emotions shift in a dramatic way that often seems to make no sense (especially to your partner). Your responses to your partner shift and the relationship dance changes.

When this happens, we are responding to an attachment cue about the level of safety in the relationship with our partner. Our body responds with alarm, our mind begins to sort through all the negative possibilities (usually catastrophic thinking) about what this cue means for us and for our relationship. We move (often aggressively) toward or away from our partner. We are usually only aware of our secondary reaction to the irritation — defensively numbing out and shutting down (withdrawal) or lashing out in anger (demand). Beneath these *surface* feelings are the more telling ones, the *softer feelings*. Once we learn to identify these, we can more appropriately and calmly communicate them to our partner, fostering understanding and trust.

There are two signs that tell you when your — or your partner's — raw spot has been hit. First, there is a sudden radical shift in the emotional tone of the conversation. You and your lover were joking just a moment ago, but now one of you is upset or enraged, or conversely, aloof or chilly. You are thrown off-balance. It's as if the game changed and no one told you. The hurt partner is sending out new signals and the other tries to make sense of the change.

Second, the reaction to a perceived offense often seems way out of proportion. A plan can be thrown off course or a distraction takes a partner's attention away from the other, and it seems like the issue becomes a mountainous catastrophe.

Most of us are afraid that if we reveal our raw spots, others will be able to control us, hurt us anytime they wish, or despise us for being vulnerable. The trouble is that our partner cannot respond to our hurts and fears if we can never speak them. To reveal our softest feelings takes courage. Here we will practice identifying these softer feelings, learning to share our vulnerabilities and raw spots and present them in a way that your partner can internalize and address them in the future.

CHECKPOINT

When a raw spot is hit...

...there is a radical shift in emotional tone.

...the response may seem way out of proportion — even to you!

...you might feel off-balance — instant shift into survival mode — you step into a spiral.

...there is often no map — you feel out of control — your feelings get scary or cue shame.

Making sense of raw spots and handling them well is key to breaking the power of the Demon Dialogues at moments of disconnection.

WORKSHEET: Recognizing When a Raw Spot Is Rubbed

Think of a moment when your raw spot was rubbed. Did you get defensive when your partner asked whether you made a withdrawal from the bank, or insult your partner after your request for something fell on deaf ears? Or, like me, were your partner's drooping eyes seen as a signal for their disinterest and disregard? What happened to your body? You might have felt spacey, detached, hot, breathless, tight in the chest, small, empty, shaky, tearful, or cold.

One client said, "I just get all agitated. I react like a cat thrown in a tub of water. What my partner sees is me being mad. But deep down that agitated feeling is more like shaky, scared."

What did your brain decide about the meaning of all this? What did you say to yourself when this happened? Did you make it a catastrophe?

Another client put it this way: "In my head I said to myself, 'she's judging me.'"

Partner 1:

Now consider the cue that triggered you, your initial response, and whether it was actually the true emotion you were feeling.

In my head I said to myself, _____

_____.

What did you do then? How did you move into action? Did you yell, accuse, or walk out of the room? You can say, "I yelled and shouted," "I left the house," or "I threw the paper towel roll at them." Now include your action:

I _____

_____.

Tie all these elements together by filling in the blanks below:

In this incident, the trigger made me feel _____.

On the surface, I probably showed _____.

But deep down, I just felt _____.
(Pick one of the basic negative emotions, e.g., *sadness, anger, shame, fear.*)

What I longed for was _____.

The main message I got about our bond, about me, or my

love was _____.

Partner 2:

Now consider the cue that triggered you, your initial response, and whether it was actually the true emotion you were feeling.

In my head I said to myself, _____

_____

What did you do then? How did you move into action? Did you yell, accuse, or walk out of the room? You can say, "I yelled and shouted," "I left the house," or "I threw the paper towel roll at them." Now include your action:

I _____

_____

Tie all these elements together by filling in the blanks below:

In this incident, the trigger made me feel _____.

On the surface, I probably showed _____.

But deep down, I just felt _____.
(Pick one of the basic negative emotions, e.g., *sadness, anger, shame, fear*.)

What I longed for was _____.

The main message I got about our bond, about me, or my

love was _____.

LET'S GET INTROSPECTIVE:
Journal Exercise

Because our fears and attachment patterns stem from past relationships, you may find you are not ready or able to articulate your raw spots. For this exercise, take some time individually to reflect and revisit some of the ways in which your raw spots developed. Perhaps go for a walk in nature to avoid distractions and be gentle with yourself. Record your memories and feelings about a raw spot below. You might need several days as you open doors to people and places you might have long closed, or at least that you thought you'd closed but that have come back knocking to disturb your current relationship.

Consider the following and note your responses as you learn to identify and articulate your raw spot.

Your history: Did your raw spot arise in your relationship with your parents, your siblings, in another romantic relationship, or even in your relationships with your peers as you grew up? Or is it a sensitivity that was born in your current relationship?

....

....

....

....

....

....

....

....

....

Your partner: Do you think your partner sees this vulnerability in you? Or do they just see the reactive surface feeling or the action response?

....

....

....

....

....

....

....

Flip the script: Can you guess one of your partner's raw spots? Do you know exactly what you do to irritate them?

_____

_____

_____

_____

_____

_____

_____

_____

_____

We want and need our lovers to respond to our hurt, but they can't do that if we don't express it. Are you preventing your lover from getting close? You will never create a strong, secure connection if you do not allow your lover to know you fully, or if your lover is unwilling to know you. The following list of statements can help you see if you are exhibiting actions that keep your lover at arm's length, preventing your raw spots from being agitated.

MARK EACH OF THE FOLLOWING STATEMENTS AS TRUE OR FALSE:

1. I find that I hold on to anger, because   **T**   **F**
   that is an emotion I feel is more easily
   expressed.

2. I am afraid to cry because if I start,   **T**   **F**
   I may not stop.

3. If I share my raw spot or my soft   **T**   **F**
   feelings, then it might give my partner
   ammunition against me or expose me
   in some way my partner may exploit.

4. Feeling hurt is a waste of time. It doesn't   **T**   **F**
   get anyone anywhere.

5. Feeling hurt will keep me in a low place   **T**   **F**
   of continuous hurt, and I don't have
   time for that.

6. I am afraid my partner might find me   **T**   **F**
   unattractive if I show frailty.

7. When my partner shows signs of   **T**   **F**
   distress, I often feel overwhelmed and
   ignore them instead of responding
   to them.

WORSHEET: Finding the Raw Spots

Individually, write your responses to the following questions to find your raw spots.

Partner 1:
Identify a specific moment during a fight or time of distance when you suddenly felt more vulnerable or on guard.

_____

_____

_____

What is the most negative thought that went through your head? What is the worst, most catastrophic thought you had about your partner, yourself, and your relationship when you remember that moment? (For example, *They just didn't care. I was just never going to make it right. We were going to fight and split up.*)

_____

_____

_____

Pick the word that best describes the softer feeling (deeper emotion) that came up for you in that moment (e.g., *scared, inadequate, failing, ashamed, isolated*). A word that comes to mind for you will often be some kind of fear about yourself or your partner and how they feel about you. It may be some kind of anguish or hurt.

In that moment of disconnection, deep down I felt _____ _____.

During this past incident, did you show you felt this way? If not, what feeling did you show? (Most often when we feel unsafe, we show anger, frustration, or no feeling at all.)

_____

_____

_____

What did you learn from responding to these questions?

_____

_____

_____

_____

Partner 2:

Identify a specific moment during a fight or time of distance when you suddenly felt more vulnerable or on guard.

_____

_____

_____

_____

What is the most negative thought that went through your head? What is the worst, most catastrophic thought you had about your partner, yourself, and your relationship when you remember that moment? (For example, *They just didn't care. I was just never going to make it right. We were going to fight and split up.*)

_____

_____

_____

_____

Pick the word that best describes the softer feeling (deeper emotion) that came up for you in that moment (e.g., *scared, inadequate, failing, ashamed, isolated*). A word that comes to mind for you will often be some kind of fear about yourself or your partner and how they feel about you. It may be some kind of anguish or hurt.

In that moment of disconnection, deep down I felt _____

_____ .

During this past incident, did you show you felt this way? If not, what feeling did you show? (Most often when we feel unsafe, we show anger, frustration, or no feeling at all.)

_____

_____

_____

What did you learn from responding to these questions?

_____

_____

_____

Fill in the blanks below and share with one another.

Partner 1:

When we get stuck in our Demon Dialogue I often show you

_____ but underneath I feel _____.

It feels _____ to tell you this right now.

If you wanted to help me with this feeling you could

_____

_____

Partner 2:

When we get stuck in our Demon Dialogue I often show you

_____ but underneath I feel _____.

It feels _____ to tell you this right now.

If you wanted to help me with this feeling you could

_____

_____

WORKSHEET: Identifying the Feelings Beneath the Surface

When we feel vulnerable, often the way we act or the things we say are not what is at the heart of the matter. Catastrophizing, reacting with hypersensitivity, or having a knee-jerk reaction is what is presented on the surface, known as *surface feelings.* But underneath is real fear, so identifying our *softer feelings* — those that are lying beneath the surface of our actions and words, our responses and reaction — can help us communicate our fears much more effectively to one another. An individual might have a surface feeling of hostility, for instance, but underneath can feel ignored (softer feeling); another can be overly accommodating on the surface but feel resentful deep down (softer feeling). In many cases, the surface feeling is saying one thing but means another.

Can you both pinpoint a recurring moment when an alarm sounds for you? What is the surface feeling or behavior you tend to exhibit? What is the softer feeling that comes up for you?

Circle your softer feelings below.

In moments of disconnection, deep down I feel:

Lonely	Dismissed
Unimportant	Helpless
Scared	Hurt
Hopeless	Intimidated
Panicked	Rejected
Inadequate	Sad
Failing	Ashamed
Lost	Confused
Isolated	Let down
Humiliated	Small/Insignificant
Overwhelmed	Unwanted
Vulnerable	Worried/Shaky

Partner 1:

In these moments, my most vulnerable feeling is _____

_____

_____

and my worst (catastrophic) thought is (e.g. *You will want to break up, you will cheat on me, you will find me unattractive.*)

Partner 2:

In these moments, my most vulnerable feeling is _____

_____

_____

and my worst (catastrophic) thought is _____.
(e.g. *You will want to break up, you will cheat on me, you will find me unattractive.*)

If this exercise is too hard for you, then try sharing with your partner your uncertainty about this kind of confiding.

Can you think of a time when you shared a sense of vulnerability or a hurt feeling with your partner and they responded in a way that helped you feel close? What did your lover do that really made a difference? Perhaps you were hugged or called a special name.

Partner 1:

_____

_____

_____

_____

_____

Partner 2:

_____

_____

_____

_____

_____

Can you agree on a typical recent interaction where you both felt disconnected and ended up stuck for a while in a Demon Dialogue? In this situation, who turned up the emotional heat or tried to turn it down by exhibiting surface behaviors to avoid strong emotions? Come up with a phrase to describe how you usually deal with your partner (e.g., *get icy, get into battle mode, run and hide*).

Partner 1:

My phrase: _____

_____

_____

_____

Partner 2:

My phrase: _____

_____

_____

_____

_____

If you habitually react in this way, it is probably because it seemed like the only viable option for you in past relationships. How did this way of dealing with emotion work to keep the most important relationships in your life intact? For example, did your approach help to get a loved one's attention or make them less obviously rejecting or unresponsive?

Partner 1:

_____

_____

_____

_____

Partner 2:

_____

_____

_____

_____

In the recent interaction with your partner, did you stay with surface, reactive feelings or were you eventually able to explore and share deeper, softer feelings? Rate the following statements on a scale of one to five, where one indicates that you strongly disagree and five indicates that you strongly agree. Share your answers with your partner.

Partner 1:
Disagree/Agree (circle a number)

1 2 3 4 5 I want to talk about my more vulnerable emotions right now.

1 2 3 4 5 I have fearful thoughts about sharing these emotions.

1 2 3 4 5 It was a relief to pinpoint your emotion and open with it.

Partner 2:

Disagree/Agree (circle a number)

1 2 3 4 5   I want to talk about my more vulnerable emotions right now.

1 2 3 4 5   I have fearful thoughts about sharing these emotions.

1 2 3 4 5   It was a relief to pinpoint your emotion and open with it.

When you think of this interaction where you got stuck as a couple, can you each identify the cue that had you lose your emotional balance and spin into raw insecurity? For instance, one person forgot about a planned event, causing the other to slam the door and attend the event alone.

Partner 1:

_____

_____

_____

_____

_____

_____

Partner 2:

_____

_____

_____

_____

_____

_____

Share with your partner your catastrophic thinking.

When I think of sharing my softest feelings with you here, it is hard to do. I worry the following will happen:

Partner 1:

_____

_____

_____

_____

_____

Partner 2:

_____

_____

_____

_____

_____

Ask your partner how they feel when you share this way. How do they help you feel safe enough to share? What impact do you both feel this kind of sharing has on the relationship?

Partner 1:

_____

_____

_____

_____

Partner 2:

_____

_____

_____

_____

_____

Can you create, together, a new version of that difficult interaction you began this exercise with? Can you each, in turn, describe the surface way you moved in that dance but using your softer feelings? For example, "I moved in my dance by shutting down and avoiding and I felt uncomfortable and on edge, like I wanted to get away," or "I felt ticked off and dismissed."

Partner 1:

I moved in my dance by _____ ,

_____

and I felt _____

_____ .

Partner 2:

I moved in my dance by _____,

_____

and I felt _____

_____.

Now we can go a little deeper. Try to add the specific attachment cue that sparked the powerful emotions you circled in the list of softer feelings on page 79. Perhaps it was something you thought you heard in your partner's voice or that you didn't receive a card for your birthday. Then add the feelings that you circled.

Partner 1:

When I heard/saw _____

[attachment cue], I just felt _____

[softer feeling].

Partner 2:

When I heard/saw _____

[attachment cue], I just felt _____

[softer feeling].

Try to stay with simple, concrete language. Big, ambiguous words or labels scramble this conversation. If you get stuck, just share that with one another, try to go back to the last place that was clear, and start again.

Now we can put all these elements together.

Partner 1:

When we get stuck in our cycle and I _____

[use an action word, e.g., *push*], I feel _____

[surface feeling]. The emotional trigger for my sense of dis-

connection is when I see/sense/hear _____

[*attachment cue*]. On a deeper level, I am feeling _____

_____

[*softer feeling*]. It is _____

[e.g. *hard/easy, pleasurable/scary, strange/comfortable*] to

tell you this. If you want to help me with this feeling, then

right now you could _____

[e.g. *hold me, engage with me, tell me you love me*].

Partner 2:

When we get stuck in our cycle and I _____

[use an action word, e.g., *push*], I feel _____

[surface feeling]. The emotional trigger for my sense of dis-

connection is when I see/sense/hear _____

[*attachment cue*]. On a deeper level, I am feeling _____

_____

[*softer feeling*]. It is _____

[e.g. *hard/easy, pleasurable/scary, strange/comfortable*] to

tell you this. If you want to help me with this feeling, then

right now you could _____

[e.g. *hold me, engage with me, tell me you love me*].

What did each of you just learn about the other person's raw spots? Share your answers with one another. See if you can validate one another for the risks you've both taken by being open and honest.

Partner 1:

_____

_____

_____

_____

_____

_____

Partner 2:

_____

_____

_____

_____

_____

In any interaction, even if both of you are paying attention, you cannot be tuned in all the time. Signals get missed, and there will be moments when attachment vulnerability takes center stage. The secret is to recognize and deal with raw spots in ways that don't get you into negative patterns. In the next chapter, you will learn more about how to work with these attachment feelings to de-escalate the destructive patterns we fall into.

Hold These Tight

....

- In love, sharing even negative emotions is more useful than emotional absence.
- We have surface emotions that are usually our first reactions, but beneath are the softer feelings that indicate the vulnerabilities or raw spots that have been exposed.
- It is hard to tune in to raw spots because our surface emotions distract us and our partners from what we are really afraid of.
- Making sense of raw spots and handling them well is key to breaking the power of Demon Dialogues at moments of disconnection.

Revisiting a Rocky Moment

All couples argue. Some couples can cut short a fight and change direction because on most days, their relationship is a safe haven of loving responsiveness. People who feel secure with their partner find it easier to do this. They can stand back and reflect on the process between them, and they can also own their part in that process. For distressed lovers, this is much harder to do. They are caught up in the emotional chaos at the surface of the relationship, in seeing one another as threats, as the enemy.

To reconnect, lovers have to be able to de-escalate the conflict and actively create a basic emotional safety. They need to be able to work in concert to curtail their negative dialogues and defuse their fundamental insecurities. They may not be as close as they crave to be, but they can stop stepping on one another's toes. They can have their differences and not careen helplessly into Demon Dialogues. They can rub one another's raw spots and not slide into anxious demands or numbing withdrawal. They can deal better with the disorienting ambiguity that their loved one, who is the solution to fear, can also suddenly become a source of fear. In short, they can hold on to their emotional balance a lot more often and a lot more easily. This creates a platform for repairing rifts in their relationship and creating a truly loving connection.

> ## CHECKPOINT: Revisiting a Rocky Moment
>
> *The focus is:*
> - Recalling Demon Dialogue patterns
> - Remembering Raw Spots
> - Repairing rifts
> - Rising above the negative cycle
> - Reframing the cycle so your partner is not the enemy

DE-ESCALATING DISCONNECTION

We can all recall a drama we encountered with our partners. There is always a pivotal point where the Demon Dialogue sets in and the conversation turns contentious, taking on a life of its own. Up to now, we've discussed and determined why and how this happens, which means we now have the tools to create a new kind of dance. Here are the steps that can set you on the path to greater harmony, when you're in the thick of it.

Step 1: Seeing and Stopping the Dance. This involves moving from, "You are attacking and hurting me," or "No, you are shutting me out and dismissing me," to "We are trapped here."

Step 2: Claiming Your Own Moves. You have learned to do this in previous chapters, in both *Before the Conversations* and *Conversation #1: Recognizing the Demon Dialogues*. It helps when partners can agree upon names to describe these moves.

Step 3: Claiming Your Own Feelings. You have learned to do this in *Conversation #2: Finding the Raw Spots*. It is best to start with surface reactive feelings and then to admit to the deeper, softer feelings. We can be angry on the surface and hurt and vulnerable on a deeper level. It's important to remember that these tsunami emotions are just a part of love. We all struggle with them, but we can start owning them.

Step 4: Owning How You Shape Your Partner's Feelings. We have enormous impact on our partners. It is still hard for most of us to really grasp this, especially if we are used to hearing only surface signals from our loved one. For most of us, it is a relief that we do impact our partner, but then this is also a responsibility. Our partner does have to help us here. We cannot rely on guesswork.

Step 5: Asking About Our Partner's Deeper Emotions. You have begun to listen to and hopefully explore your own and your partner's deeper emotions in Conversation #2. In that chapter, you hopefully became more comfortable with this process of vulnerability. It helps to have the framework that tells us what the emotional landscape of love is like and names the normal fears and longings that all of us have.

Step 6: Sharing Your Deeper Emotions. You became more familiar with acknowledging and naming the emotions you have discovered through Demon Dialogues and raw spots, and now you can validate them through revisiting a Rocky Moment. Each time we do this, we become more comfortable and our emotions become clearer and so, less overwhelming.

Step 7: Standing Together. This is the endgame. You can now come back to common ground even after emotion earthquakes have occurred. When you can do it, it is so powerful that it offers you a platform of safety, a secure base in your relationship from which to launch into a positive Hold Me Tight conversation, which is coming up in the next chapter. You can help one another find an exit from Demon Dialogues and feel safe.

LET'S GET INTROSPECTIVE:
Journal Exercise

Revisit a previous Rocky Moment when you became stuck in your own Demon Dialogue. Use the steps above and write a story of how you could have contained the momentum of your negative cycle and created a base of safety instead.

....

....

....

....

....

....

....

....

....

SELF-CARE DURING ROCKY MOMENTS

It is during this Conversation #3 when I usually check in with how each partner is feeling about the process thus far. It is also around this time when couples have enough of the Hold Me Tight experience under their belts that they can begin to assess how they are feeling toward one another, and especially with themselves. I typically take their temperature at this point, asking whether they feel hopeful, fruitless, or satisfied with their progress. It is with no ego, but just science to back me, that I can proudly say most of the check-ins are positive. That is the magic of EFT—the science- and research-proven approach to couples therapy. But it can't ever hurt to check in with yourself!

The following worksheet is designed for both of you to reflect on the work done so far, assess how you're feeling, and share your reflections with one another. Even if your answers might not seem as encouraging as you'd like, make this an opportunity to discuss them with your partner and revisit them every so often. None of this work is futile, even if that feels like your mindset right now; it can be utilized and referred to as you are both conducting important research about your needs, fears, and the bond you have together.

WORKSHEET: Taking the Temperature of Your Hold Me Tight Journey

Partner 1:

How are you feeling? (For example, did you wake up feeling a sense of foreboding? Do you feel refreshed? Are you excited about something or eager to do something or see someone?)

_____

_____

_____

_____

If you are feeling down or happy, what is making you feel that way? (You might say, "I am feeling happy because I woke up realizing I was holding my partner for the first time in a long while.")

_____

_____

_____

_____

What is *not* working for you? (For example, "The pace of my workload is not ideal.")

_____

_____

_____

_____

What *is* working for you? (You might say, "Asking for help," or, "Date night with my significant other.")

_____

_____

_____

_____

What are you proud of? (For example, "I defused an argument this week," or, "Being together felt light and very natural.")

_____

_____

_____

_____

What's occupying your mental real estate these days? (You might say, "An impending overnight visit by a relative," "A deadline at work," or, "My partner's birthday present.")

_____

_____

_____

_____

Do you feel like you're in a rut? If so, why?

_____

_____

_____

Is there one way you can have fun today or this week? (For example, going for a massage, coloring with your child, or reaching out to an old friend for an old-fashioned phone call.)

_____

_____

_____

Can you learn from a mistake or faux pas you made this week? What is the lesson? How can you be grateful for the mistake and make the lesson enhance your life? (For example, maybe you made a joke that offended someone or didn't validate your partner's stress by actively listening to an account about an incident.)

_____

_____

_____

_____

_____

What inspires you? (Is it a sunset, your pet, reading about a contemporary hero?)

_____

_____

_____

_____

What can you forgive yourself for? (You might tell yourself that it's okay that you made an offending joke; you didn't mean any harm and you now know better.)

_____

_____

What can you thank yourself for? (Maybe you volunteered today, or made your partner happy by saying something loving and unsolicited.)

_____

_____

Are you following anyone on social media who makes you feel insecure, inadequate, and generally terrible about yourself or your relationship and family?

_____

_____

What is becoming tiresome? What can you do about that?
(For example, maybe you are tired of your evening ritual or
a certain toxic friend. Can you create a new ritual or set
better boundaries with those who exude negativity?)

_____

_____

_____

_____

Partner 2:

How are you feeling? (For example, did you wake up
feeling a sense of foreboding? Do you feel refreshed? Are
you excited about something or eager to do something or
see someone?)

_____

_____

_____

_____

If you are feeling down or happy, what is making you feel that way? (You might say, "I am feeling happy because I woke up realizing I was holding my partner for the first time in a long while.")

_____

_____

_____

What is *not* working for you? (For example, "The pace of my workload is not ideal.")

_____

_____

_____

What *is* working for you? (You might say, "Asking for help," or, "Date night with my significant other.")

_____

_____

_____

What are you proud of? (For example, "I defused an argument this week," or, "Being together felt light and very natural.")

_____

_____

_____

_____

What's occupying your mental real estate these days? (You might say, "An impending overnight visit by a relative," "A deadline at work," or, "My partner's birthday present.")

_____

_____

_____

_____

Do you feel like you're in a rut? If so, why?

_____

_____

_____

_____

Is there one way you can have fun today or this week? (For example, going for a massage, coloring with your child, or reaching out to an old friend for an old-fashioned phone call.)

_____

_____

_____

_____

_____

Can you learn from a mistake or faux pas you made this week? What is the lesson? How can you be grateful for the mistake and make the lesson enhance your life? (For example, maybe you made a joke that offended someone or didn't validate your partner's stress by actively listening to an account about an incident.)

_____

_____

_____

_____

What inspires you? (Is it a sunset, your pet, reading about a contemporary hero?)

_____

_____

_____

What can you forgive yourself for? (You might tell yourself that it's okay that you made an offending joke; you didn't mean any harm and you now know better.)

_____

_____

_____

What can you thank yourself for? (Maybe you volunteered today, or made your partner happy by saying something loving and unsolicited.)

_____

_____

_____

Are you following anyone on social media who makes you feel insecure, inadequate, and generally terrible about yourself or your relationship and family?

_____

_____

_____

What is becoming tiresome? What can you do about that? (For example, maybe you are tired of your evening ritual or a certain toxic friend. Can you create a new ritual or set better boundaries with those who exude negativity?)

_____

_____

_____

EFT is an ongoing process. It's not something to read about or do in a workbook and then toss aside. It is here for you, not just now or during inevitable rocky moments, but as a booster to your future relationship—the one you have carved out together through doing this critical work. These questions are the beginning of a self-care journey that will only benefit your partner and all your relationships in the long run.

Hold These Tight
....

- Revisiting Rocky Moments incorporates identifying Demon Dialogues and Raw Spots.
- The essence of repair is to be able to slow down and change the level of conversation.
- Partners rise above negative cycles and see the pattern and how it victimizes them.
- Both partners are more and more able to see how they both get stuck in the dance of disconnection and how this dance is their common enemy.

Hold Me Tight — Engaging and Connecting

Deep romantic gazes, slow dancing in perfect synchrony, losing time in one another's embraces. These are not the behaviors merely reserved for new lovers in a Nicholas Sparks novel. Moments of intoxicating connection, intense responsiveness, and unflinching engagement can be and should be vital throughout the lifetime of a relationship. Indeed, they are the hallmarks of happy, secure couples.

When we are falling in love, almost all of us are naturally and spontaneously tuned in to our partners. We are hyperaware of one another and exquisitely sensitive to our partner's every action and word, every expression of feeling. But with time, many of us become less attentive, more complacent, and even jaded with our partners. Our emotional antennas get jammed, or maybe our partner's signals get weaker. Where there was once attunement, disharmony takes over.

To build and sustain a secure bond, we need to be able to tune back in to our loved one as strongly as we did before. How do we do this? By deliberately creating moments of engagement and connection, of mutual understanding and safety. In the Hold Me Tight conversation, you can build on the sense of safety that you and your partner have already started to create as a result of the previous three conversations. So far in the journey, you have been taught how to halt or contain negative patterns of interacting with your partner, as well as mark and name at least one of the deeper feelings that come up in negative cycles and moments of disconnection. Effectively seeking connection and responding supportively is hard without a basic platform of safety. But as I mentioned in *Hold Me Tight* if Conversations #1, #2, and #3 are like going for a walk in the park together, Conversation #4 is like dancing the tango.

Here you'll learn how to generate positive patterns of *reaching for* and *responding to* your loved one. This is a conversation that helps reinforce the benefits of vulnerability. As both partners learn to share and respond more compassionately, they create more positive feelings toward one another, which naturally encourages a cycle of more open communication and even more deeply attuned responses to one another's fears and needs. In effect, you'll be learning how to speak one another's language of attachment.

Understanding and communicating fears and needs are at the root of Conversation #4, which has two questions to consider. The first question — *What Am I Most Afraid Of?* — requires further exploring and elaborating on the deeper feelings you touched on with the previous conversations. In those dialogues, you were taking the elevator down into your emotions. To discover your attachment priorities, you must now — through asking your-self, "What am I most afraid of?" — go all the way to the basement.

The second question — *What Do I Need Most from You?* — is the crucial encounter in Emotionally Focused Therapy. It involves being able to openly and coherently speak your needs in a way that invites your partner into a new dialogue marked by **accessibility, responsiveness,** and **engagement,** or an A.R.E. conversation, which we discussed in the first chapter. Generally, this kind of A.R.E. interaction is the basis of effective dependency: the dependency that offers a secure base with a loved one.

Both questions challenge couples to confront the elements of their conversations, which can reveal:

- What each person is afraid of.
- What each person longs for from a partner.
- How easy it is for each person to speak their fears.
- How easy it is for each person to ask for what they need from their partner.

The ability to engage in this conversation is based on the safety that you both have created in the first three conversations. The Hold Me Tight conversation and the two questions within it are immensely rewarding for couples and offer an antidote to Demon Dialogues and moments of deprivation and desertion. In this conversation, the more withdrawn partner moves closer, moving from a powerless position and closing the gap of distance between them. This partner becomes engaged. The more blaming partner, therefore, moves away from a controlling position. This partner enters a softer emotional state, reaching for closeness in a positive way. Withdrawers re-engage, while blamers soften.

The reason that these kinds of interactions are so positive is probably that they turn on the cuddle hormone oxytocin. This hormone produces a sense of calm contentment and facilitates bonding. It also increases our tendency to trust another person. Oxytocin is a key factor in the chemistry of love. It is part of the bliss of orgasm and of breastfeeding a baby.

When we can tune in to and respond to a loved one in an A.R.E. manner, we can intuit one another's intentions and realities, and dance as one. This means that we must learn to do two things: disclose our feelings, as well as attend to our partner's disclosures. The idea is that once a disclosing partner feels attended to in a safe and loving way, the deeper both partners can move into their feelings and communicate them more clearly. EFT researchers have found that when couples can do this, they can solve problems and bridge differences together as a team. This is not only because they feel safer, but also because problems are no longer barometers of love and belonging; they are just problems.

PUT A CHECK BESIDE ANY OF THE HABITS THAT FEEL FAMILIAR:

- ☐ Finding a chore not done and moving into, "You didn't do . . . You just don't listen and you don't care about me at all."
- ☐ Finding a difference of opinion and making it a relational issue, as in, "You don't want to build the shelves the way I asked so you just dismiss me and my wishes. If you cared about me . . ."
- ☐ Taking a momentary mismatch in intimacy and making it into a verdict, as in, "You fell asleep after we agreed to make love on Saturday night, so this means our agreements mean nothing and we are losing all our sexiness."

> **CHECKPOINT: Terms of Endearment**
>
> The word *attend* comes from the Latin *ad tendere*, which means *to reach toward.* We want to reach toward one another, and the Hold Me Tight conversation helps partners do just that.

QUESTION 1:
WHAT AM I MOST AFRAID OF?

This part of the conversation is aimed at gaining greater emotional clarity. It is during this conversation that partners become able to declare their core attachment fears, which naturally leads to a recognition of their primary attachment needs, addressed in Question 2: What Do I Most Need From You? How can you take the insights you've already gained about your needs, fears, and behaviors and go deeper to the basement of your deepest vulnerability? What this looks like is going from "I feel scared when you walk away from me," to "I'm sad because it seems we cannot connect anymore." The first statement, while certainly valid and honest, doesn't specifically communicate the fear. The second focuses on what being walked away from represents — the fear of not connecting.

Even after expressing their feelings throughout the first three conversations, partners are always amazed at the potential to hit the elevator button and go even farther down. Fear and vulnerability are not the same thing. Getting to the vulnerability that makes us afraid is the key to this conversation. To do this, I teach my couples how to use *handles*. Handles are descriptive images, words, and phrases that open the door to your innermost feelings and vulnerabilities: your emotional reality.

HOLD ME TIGHT HANDLES

Handles aren't just for long-haul truck drivers with their CB radios. Therapists use handles for several reasons. First, handles create momentum. They are useful when resuming a conversation from a prior session. Usually, you'll hear a therapist say something like, "Last week you were feeling trapped." The word "trapped" is the handle that acts as an anchor for both therapist and patient. Recently I spoke with a patient who blurted out, "I feel like I'm walking through fire." This image evokes so many sensations, which themselves are anchors that keep us in touch with our fears, not only as they manifest emotionally, but through the physical sensations they produce.

And speaking of anchoring, handles help anchor us to our deeper fears. They not only remind us of something that might have triggered a fear but keep us rooted in our vulnerability. Learning to use handles and to call upon them when we might feel we are at a loss for words can help facilitate effective language and better serve the listening partner because the feelings are clear. Because of the imagery often used in handles, our bodies naturally react to those images. Partners can learn to look for signs of stress and fear through recognizing the change in their partner's body language when vulnerability takes over. This is how we learn to read our partners and prepare to respond with compassion instead of being led by our own fears.

The following are handles that might help you as you learn to use language that exposes your vulnerability.

INSTEAD OF SAYING...	TRY THE HANDLE...
I don't feel in control.	I'm freaking out.
I don't know what to do.	I feel overwhelmed.
I feel all alone.	My heart is shattered.
I can't sleep or shut my thoughts down.	I feel anxious.
I don't want to be here.	I want to flee.
I can't take the pressure.	It feels like walking through fire.
I am confused beyond belief.	It feels like my head is exploding.
I feel sad and unmotivated.	I feel like a slug in mud.

WORKSHEET: What's Your Handle?

Now it's your turn. Can you turn your feelings into a more vulnerable handle? Remember your handle doesn't have to be an action; it can be an image or a phrase. The idea is to have your handle be something you remember and can call upon to anchor you when you are slipping into a Demon Dialogue. Check in with your body. Do you notice any changes that you can identify as signals to how you are feeling? For instance, when you share your handle, do you notice your leg shaking or foot wagging? Do you begin playing with your hair or picking at your fingernails? The next time you notice one of these physical changes, you can ask yourself, "Is this my handle talking?"

Partner 1:

My feelings _____

_____

My handle _____

_____

My body language _____

_____

Partner 2:

My feelings _____

_____

My handle _____

_____

My body language _____

_____

When you feel like you can name and be specific about your main fear, see if you can imagine saying this to your partner before you actually do. Then see if you can share this in a simple short form with your partner. If this is hard, then just go slow. You can let it trickle out or ask your partner to go first. Sharing handles is like shorthand for understanding one another. It doesn't have to feel burdensome. Learning this new language can feel like a relief.

QUESTION 2:
WHAT DO I NEED MOST FROM YOU?

Going deeper by using handles helps us move into and lay out the emotions that are at the center of our longing for safe connection. When a partner begins to communicate their needs, they become the disclosing partner.

Having a partner suddenly disclose vulnerabilities can be hard for the listening partner to hear or to trust. I have heard partners dismiss their lover's new steps toward them with everything from, "That's ridiculous" to some version of "So let's see you prove it." Then they spin back into their Demon Dialogue.

The truth is, no one takes the risk of being rebuffed by disclosing unless the other person really matters to them. And sometimes disclosing partners have to be willing to hang in there and keep repeating their message until their loved one gets used to seeing them in a new way. Couples stuck in a Demon Dialogue can also get moving again by repeating Conversations #1, #2, and #3.

What follows is a sample script of how partners take turns disclosing and responding in a way that reinforces mutual responsiveness and engagement, the two facets of *attending*.

WORSHEET: Practicing Identifying Handles

See if you can identify the handles each partner uses in this sample dialogue between Micah and Taylor. Circle words that resonate and those that help go deeper.

Micah: When you came home late, I told you I was upset, and you said, "Now don't get all crazy on me," and that if my outbursts didn't stop, you might need to leave. That threat was the bottom line for me. I cannot always stay calm and logical.

Taylor: Sorry.

Micah: I feel very sad we cannot seem to come together anymore.

Taylor: But you shouldn't be because we are working on our relationship. What was the worst moment, the worst feeling for you? [You might recognize this question from *Conversation #3: Revisiting a Rocky Moment*.]

Micah: [Sits, thinking.]

Taylor: I only say you are crazy because I get scared of the bad feelings between us.

Micah: The worst moments were when you hung up on me, and later when you said you would leave. I was so "unreasonable," you said.

Taylor: I don't know how to make this better. What should I do?

Micah: I just want to know if you care that you hurt my feelings. If I get scared or upset with you, you just turn off, like you're hanging up on me. You don't comfort me. And you don't make love to me or hold me, either. Just when I need you, you go off in your disapproval. You turn away and discard me. I am not the person you want.

Taylor: [Sits quietly.]

Micah: It kills me when you pass over me, turn to your rules. I have never been more alone. Taylor, you are not there for me, with me. So I panic. Do you hear me?

Taylor: [Reaching for Micah's hands.] Yes, yes, yes. This is sad to hear. I'm sad.

Taylor *is* sad. Taylor's emotional presence is as tangible as the chair Taylor sits on. Micah has revealed a deep pain, the primal code of loss and panic that sounds when our loved one is not there for us, and they have heard one another. Both partners have connected with their own emotional realities and opened up to one another.

LET'S GET INTROSPECTIVE:
Journal Exercise

Vulnerability is painful to experience. It's even more difficult to articulate. Sharing fears with our partner takes trust and understanding. I often begin by asking couples to think of a secure attachment figure from their past: a parent, a lover, a close friend.

Then I ask, "If you were to share with this person your deepest vulnerability, the fear that you can't seem to let escape from your mouth, what would it be?" Answers might be "I'm afraid I'll be alone," "I can't seem to forgive myself," or "I'm afraid that will happen to me again."

Then I ask, "What kind of response would you expect from this secure attachment figure?"

For this journal exercise, on your own, focus on a past secure relationship; again, this could be a parent or a close friend. Imagine that person is in front of you. How would you describe your vulnerability now? For instance, are you less scared and more clear about it? Or still unclear and fuzzy? Do you feel so strange you can hardly do it, even in your imagination? Remember your handle if you are having difficulty putting this into words.

PARTNER 1:

....

....

....

....

....

....

Now, consider a past relationship where you did not feel securely connected. Maybe you had a best friend in high school who excluded you from social activities, making you feel abandoned or outcast, not enough or less than enough. What was it you really needed from this person? Acceptance? Reassurance? Non-judgment? Write to this person now, in two sentences or less, what you needed. Take note of your body's movement, posture, or internal sensations, like tingling, heat, or butterflies in the stomach.

....

....

....

....

Moving on to your relationship with your current partner, think about what you most need in order to feel secure and loved. Write it here. The Worksheet following this exercise will help you to begin this conversation with your partner.

PARTNER 2:

....

....

....

....

....

Now, consider a past relationship where you did not feel securely connected. Maybe you had a best friend in high school who excluded you from social activities, making you feel abandoned or outcast, not enough, or less than enough. What was it you really needed from this person? Acceptance? Reassurance? Non-judgment? Write to this person now, in two sentences or less, what you needed. Take note of your body's movement, posture, or internal sensations, like tingling, heat, or butterflies in the stomach.

....

....

....

....

Moving on to your relationship with your current partner, think about what you most need in order to feel secure and loved. Write it here. The Worksheet following this exercise will help you to begin this conversation with your partner.

WORKSHEET: Fill in the Blanks

Most everyone on the planet has been overwhelmed at one time or another by their vulnerabilities. Finding words to articulate them is a useful exercise, as once you have those words, you can communicate them in your Hold Me Tight conversation, helping your partner contextualize and anticipate your handles in your own dialogues and in your interactions with others. Having completed the preceding Worksheet and Journal Exercise, try to put into sentences the needs you have based on the things that you now recognize you are afraid of.

Fill in the blanks in these sample sentences to help you get started. The first sentence is filled in for you as a guide:

I need to feel _that I am special to you_ so I _sense that I am the number one priority in your life_.

Partner 1:

I need to feel _____,

as a partner and a lover, and that _____

is important to you.

I need to feel that I can _____

so I sense that _____.

I need to feel I can ask you to _____

    so I _____.

I need to feel _____

    so I _____.

Partner 2:

I need to feel _____,

    as a partner and a lover, and that _____

    is important to you.

I need to feel that I can _____

    so I sense that _____.

I need to feel I can ask you to _____

    so I _____.

I need to feel _____

    so I _____.

    If this is too hard to do, take a smaller step and talk about how difficult it is to explicitly formulate and state your needs. Tell your partner if there is some way they can help you with this. For instance, one might say, "You could tell me that you want to hear my needs and touch me so I feel safe." This dialogue contains the key emotional drama of our lives, so sometimes we need to take smaller steps to gain and offer clarity.

Hold These Tight

- The Hold Me Tight conversation is a positive bonding event.
- This conversation offers an antidote to moments of disengagement and negative cycles, and enables you to face the world together as a team.
- Each time you can create moments of emotional connection, the bond between you grows stronger.

Forgiving Injuries

Whoever first made the claim, "We hurt the ones we love the most," must have definitely been in a long-term relationship. When I ask a room full of couples whether they have been on the giving or receiving end of hurt, disconnect, blame, or resentment with their partners, every hand goes up. It's impossible to be in an intimate long-term relationship without incident. Forming an attachment requires vulnerability, so it's absolutely normal that fear will rear its ugly head; it's how we respond and react that makes the difference between losing one another to our fear or using these incidents as opportunities for deeper connection.

Throughout the last four conversations, vulnerability, past hurts, and insecurities have been released and replaced with compassion, understanding, and attunement. Bad behavior has been exposed, raw spots have come to the surface, and needs have been expressed. It is inevitable that through one or several of these conversations, partners will bring up an event (as in *Conversation #3: Revisiting a Rocky Moment*), sometimes an apparently minor one, and it's as if all the oxygen has been sucked out of the room. All at once, the warm hope garnered over time is exchanged for a chilly despair. How can one small incident have this kind of overwhelming power to set us back? Clearly, it's not a minor incident. To one partner at least, it is a *grievous* event.

Over decades of research and therapy, I've discovered that certain incidents do more than just touch our raw spots or hurt our feelings. They injure us so deeply that they overturn our world. They are relationship traumas. A *trauma* is defined as a wound that plunges us into fear and helplessness, which challenges all our assumptions of predictability and control. Indeed, there is no greater trauma than to be wounded by the very people we count on to support and protect us.

In couples with an insecure bond, many transgressions can pose a threat to the future stability and trust of the couple. However, not all transgressions are equal to traumatic events. Traumatic wounds are especially severe, according to Judith Herman, professor of psychiatry at Harvard Medical School, because they involve a "violation of human connection." Throughout the last four conversations, you might have come face-to-face with a relationship trauma. You might find that bringing up something that may have happened three years ago remains very much alive as a raw spot, nixing any possibility of feeling safe enough to reach for your partner. More likely, depending on your primal panic mode, a past trauma will cause you to either lash out or retreat.

When a partner regresses into a primal panic based on a past traumatic event in the relationship, it is as if an alarm sounds, and that person has an overwhelming urge to retreat further so as to not explore the pain or fear. I call this the Never Again moment: They never again want to feel the way they felt in that original moment.

Lack of an emotionally supportive response by a loved one at a moment of threat can affect a whole relationship; it can eclipse hundreds of smaller positive events, and in one swipe demolish the security of a love relationship. The power of such incidents lies in the searing negative answer they offer to the eternal questions "Are you there for me when I am most in need?" and "Do you care about my pain?"

There isn't much room for compromise or an ambiguous answer when we feel this kind of urgent need for our loved one's support. The test is pass or fail. These moments can shatter all our positive assumptions about love itself and our loved one's dependability, beginning the fall into relationship distress or further fraying an already fragile bond. Until these incidents are confronted and resolved, true accessibility and emotional engagement are out of the question.

Partners often try to handle relationship traumas (also called *injuries*) by ignoring or burying them. That is a big mistake. Everyday hurts are easily dismissed and raw spots can fade if we stop rubbing them in Demon Dialogues, but unresolved traumas do not heal. The helplessness and fear they engender are almost indelible; they set off our survival instincts. Injured feelings break out at some point when attachment needs come to the fore. Often what we think has been forgotten has not been forgiven, and many times, the opposite is true. The only way out of these attachment injuries is to confront them and heal them together.

FORGIVENESS: THE FIRST GOAL FOR PARTNERS

Most scholars speak of *forgiveness* as a moral decision. Letting go of resentment and absolving a person's bad conduct is the right and good thing to do. But this decision alone will not restore trust and faith in the injuring person and the relationship. What partners need is a special type of healing conversation that fosters, not just forgiveness, but the willingness to trust again. Renewed trust is the ultimate goal.

Relationship injuries, when not addressed, can compound and make it more difficult over time to renew trust. The overarching lesson is to take a partner's hurt seriously and hang in and ask questions until the meaning of an incident becomes clear, even if the event seems trivial or the hurt exaggerated.

CHECKPOINT: What Forgiveness Isn't

Forgiveness has been the subject of research, debate, and confusion about its usefulness, meaning, and its role in our relationships. Many people mistake forgiveness as a free pass or an acceptance of the wrongdoing. Neither is the case. To put it in perspective, here are the misinterpretations that often prevent us from wanting to engage in the act of forgiveness. Once we realize what forgiveness is not, we can see what it is and why so many people—from scientists to philosophers to therapists—believe in its power to heal.

Forgiveness Is Not…	*Forgiveness Is…*
…for the other person's sake.	…for the sake of the person forgiving.
…forgoing accountability.	…speaking your feelings and making the other know how they made you feel.
…saying "It's okay."	…freeing oneself from expending energy of a grudge or deep resentment and malevolent feelings, like revenge.
…being a doormat or a pushover.	…feeling anger and empowering oneself to learn to let anger go.
…pretending what happened didn't happen.	…a lesson on how you'd like to be treated by others.
…easy.	…accepting that life is hard and bad things happen.
…forgetting.	…making peace with life.

WORKSHEET: Has Trust Diminished?

For this exercise, it is important to be honest and transparent about whether you are afraid to share your relationship injury because you don't trust your partner to receive it calmly (injured partner), or if you are a partner who is not sending signals of trust that show your partner you are open and compassionate enough to listen (injuring partner). For each statement, circle *Often, Sometimes,* or *Never.*

Injured partner:

I need time to muster the courage to speak about a past injury.	**Often**	**Sometimes**	**Never**
I mention I want to talk and then I change my mind.	**Often**	**Sometimes**	**Never**
I assume my partner will belittle, rage, accuse, or tell me it's all in my head.	**Often**	**Sometimes**	**Never**
When I share, I feel like my partner is making a case against me and my feelings.	**Often**	**Sometimes**	**Never**
After I share, I feel worse and more alone than before I shared.	**Often**	**Sometimes**	**Never**

I believe our private conversations are not kept private by my partner.	**Often**	**Sometimes**	**Never**
I feel physically ill, nervous, or jittery when I try to speak my mind.	**Often**	**Sometimes**	**Never**
I feel like I repeat myself over and over and my partner doesn't hear me.	**Often**	**Sometimes**	**Never**
When it comes to sharing, I think, "What's the point?"	**Often**	**Sometimes**	**Never**

Injuring partner:

My partner makes mountains out of molehills.	**Often**	**Sometimes**	**Never**
My partner makes it seem like everything is my fault.	**Often**	**Sometimes**	**Never**
My partner doesn't listen to me when I try to explain the issue.	**Often**	**Sometimes**	**Never**
I feel like I hear the same complaints over and over again.	**Often**	**Sometimes**	**Never**

I feel guilty or to blame when my partner shares with me.	**Often**	**Sometimes**	**Never**
I don't feel like I should apologize.	**Often**	**Sometimes**	**Never**
Regarding my partner sharing an incident, I feel like my partner is playing games with me.	**Often**	**Sometimes**	**Never**
When it comes to listening, I think, "What's the point?"	**Often**	**Sometimes**	**Never**

Share with your partner the statements that you believe most fit, then share how and when you each get stuck in this thought.

There may be a trust issue when it comes to sharing your experience of receiving injuries. The injured partner might feel unsupported or recall times when their sharing wasn't received in a way that felt comforting or heard. The injuring party sometimes feels too much shame and guilt to remain open, and may respond by rejecting their partner's feelings, making them feel unimportant. Being honest with one another and sharing the answers to the trust worksheet in the previous section can put you on even ground, since the feelings you have are shared by each of you but are just manifesting differently. Can you start again? Can you muster the courage to be vulnerable, to share a trauma? Can you listen quietly and carefully, hearing the hidden messages of the injured partner? These are choices and making them is one part of the forgiveness cycle. In my book, *Hold Me Tight*, a couple named Ted and Vera demonstrate the power of forgiveness and the six-step process to achieving it.

SIX STEPS TO FORGIVENESS:

1. The hurt partner needs to speak about the pain as openly and simply as possible.

2. The injuring partner stays emotionally present and acknowledges the wounded partner's pain and their role in it.

3. Together, partners start revising their script and stop the cycle of Never Again.

4. The injuring partner now takes ownership of how they inflicted this injury on their partner and expresses regret and remorse.

5. A Hold Me Tight conversation takes place, centering on the attachment injury.

6. The couple now creates a new story that captures the injuring event—how it happened, eroded trust and connection, and shaped Demon Dialogues.

Injuries may be forgiven, but they never disappear. Instead, in the best outcomes, they become integrated into couples' attachment stories as demonstrations of renewal and connection.

LET'S GET INTROSPECTIVE:
Journal Exercise

The first step in healing an attachment injury is to recognize and articulate it. Think of an incident in the past when you were hurt by someone important to you, but not your current partner. The trauma may be one that is quite significant, or less so. Was it a remark, a specific action, or a lack of action on the part of the other? What alarming conclusion did you come to about this important person in your life? For example, did you decide this person didn't care, that you weren't important and might be abandoned?

PARTNER 1:

....

....

....

....

....

....

....

Now ask yourself, what were you longing for when you were wounded? If this is hard to articulate, see if you can figure out what you think would have been the ideal response. What protective moves did you find yourself taking? For example, did you change the subject and walk out of the room? Or did you become aggressive and demand an explanation?

....

....

....

....

....

....

....

Now, ask yourself, "Did I feel deprived of support? Did my pain or fear get dismissed? Did I feel deserted? Did I feel devalued? Did I suddenly see this person as a source of danger, as taking advantage of me, or as betraying me?"

....

....

....

....

....

....

PARTNER 2:

....

....

....

....

....

....

....

....

....

Now ask yourself, what were you longing for when you were wounded? If this is hard to articulate, see if you can figure out what you think would have been the ideal response. What protective moves did you find yourself taking? For example, did you change the subject and walk out of the room? Or did you become aggressive and demand an explanation?

....

....

....

....

....

....

....

Now, ask yourself, "Did I feel deprived of support? Did my pain or fear get dismissed? Did I feel deserted? Did I feel devalued? Did I suddenly see this person as a source of danger, as taking advantage of me, or as betraying me?"

....

....

....

....

....

....

Once you have a sense of this past hurt, try to share what you've written with your partner.

SORRY — THE HARDEST WORD

Do you have a problem with apologies? Giving them? Accepting them? Both? Researchers say that's because we are predisposed to find reasons and excuses to not say sorry, because saying sorry makes us feel like underlings to the person we are apologizing to. To our survival wiring, apologizing just feels too threatening and dangerous, so we avoid it. Just like our biological predispositions for attachment, however, we can learn to overcome these intense fight-or-flight impulses. We can use our signals to help us act in more productive, communicative, compassionate ways that lead to connection.

Reflect on how easy or difficult it is for you to apologize, even in small things. Below are examples of token apologies, which can sometimes work for very small hurts, but in the case of the kind of relationship traumas and hurts we are talking about, can often increase the wounded person's pain. Can you remember a time when you voiced your regrets in any of the following ways?

PUT A CHECK MARK NEXT TO ANY YOU RECOGNIZE AND TRY TO REFRAIN FROM DEFAULTING TO THEM FOR YOUR HOLD ME TIGHT CONVERSATION.

- ☐ The four-second where-is-the-exit apology: "Yes, well, sorry 'bout that. What shall we have for dinner?"
- ☐ The minimizing responsibility apology: "Well, maybe I did that, but…"
- ☐ The forced apology: "I guess I am supposed to say…"
- ☐ The instrumental apology: "Nothing is going to work till I say this, so…"

WORKSHEET: True or False Apologies

Can you think of a time when you hurt a loved one? A time when they might have felt deprived of your support or comfort, even deserted by you? A time where you might even have seemed dangerous or rejecting to them? Can you imagine sincerely acknowledging this to them? What might you say? What might be hard for you in acknowledging the injury? Partners often use the following simple statements when they talk about having hurt a loved one. Circle **T** or **F** to indicate whether the sentiment is true or false for you.

I pulled away. I let you down. **T** **F**

I didn't see your pain and how you needed me. I was too angry, preoccupied, lost. I just shut down. **T** **F**

I didn't know what to do. I got all caught up in feeling stupid and worrying about doing the wrong thing. **T** **F**

I didn't think you'd believe that I was sorry. **T** **F**

I couldn't face how hurt you were because it made me feel ashamed that I could do that to you. **T** **F**

I was afraid of the outcome of my apologizing. What if you didn't accept it? **T** **F**

Recognizing the feelings you have about apologizing and the underlying fear you have about acknowledging your actions can help you further articulate them with your partner and use them as handles to ground you in your feelings. For a refresher on handles, see Conversation #4.

CHECKPOINT: Key Messages in Powerful Apologies

Your hurt is legitimate, understandable.
Your hurt impacts me. I care about it; it matters.
I feel sorrow, regret, even shame—I own that I hurt you.
I am here now.

LET'S GET INTROSPECTIVE:
Journal Exercise

It's time to turn to dealing with a specific injury in your current relationship. You can do this on your own or while your partner listens and tries to understand. If this sharing seems difficult, start with a relatively small recent hurt. Then, if you wish, you can repeat the exercise with a more significant hurt. Try to make it as specific as possible. Big, vague hurts are difficult to address. Perhaps you went through a difficult period when there were lots of hurt feelings. Was there one moment when that hurt crystallized? What was the trigger for the pain? What was the primary feeling? What decision did you make about the relationship, and what move did you make to protect yourself?

PARTNER 1:

_____

_____

_____

_____

_____

_____

PARTNER 2:

_____

_____

_____

_____

_____

_____

See if you can now tell your partner what you hoped for in that hurtful incident, and how it felt to not get that response. You might also share what it feels like right now to take the risk and express what you longed for. As you do this, try to avoid indicting your partner for causing you pain. That will only sabotage the conversation. As the listening partner, try to hear your partner's vulnerability and share what this evokes in you. Usually, when we really listen to someone we love who is expressing a need for us, we respond with caring.

If you are the partner who has hurt your lover, see if you can help your partner understand why you responded the way you did at the moment of injury. Think of this as a step in making your actions more predictable to your partner.

As the partner who did the hurting, can you now recognize your partner's experience, how you inflicted pain, and can you (the big A word!) apologize? This is hard to do. It takes courage to admit that we are disappointed in our own behavior; it is humbling to confess that we have been insensitive or uncaring. Perhaps we can only apologize when we allow ourselves to be moved by our loved ones' hurts and fears. If we can do this with sincerity, we are giving our loved ones a great gift.

As the injured partner, can you accept the apology? If you can, it puts the two of you on a new footing. Trust can begin to grow again. You can comfortably seek reassurance when echoes of this injury occur in the future, knowing that your partner will try to respond sensitively. And the apologizing partner can now offer the love that went astray in the original event.

Finally, sum up this conversation with your partner in a short story about the painful event, the impact it had on your relationship, and how you both recovered and intend to ensure that it doesn't happen again.

Our Short Story

_____

_____

_____

_____

_____

_____

_____

_____

Hold These Tight

- We will hurt those we love—it's how we deal with this that matters.
- Only one kind of apology works: one based on acknowledgment, sincerity, and accountability, with an effort to not repeat the behavior.
- Understanding attachment traumas and knowing that you can find and offer forgiveness if you need to gives you incredible power to create a resilient, lasting bond.

....

Bonding Through Sex and Touch

W e've been conditioned by our culture and a myriad of relationship gurus to regard passion as more of a passing sensation, rather than a durable force. We are told that the sexual fires that burned so brightly at the start of love inevitably burn down, just as our relationship, once filled with excitement, inexorably turns into prosaic friendship.

But the fact is that secure bonding and fully satisfying sexuality go hand in hand; they cue off and enhance one another. Emotional connection creates great sex, and great sex creates deeper emotional connection. When partners are emotionally accessible, responsive, and engaged, sex becomes intimate play, a safe adventure. Secure partners feel free and confident to surrender to sensation in one another's arms, explore and fulfill their sexual needs, and share their deepest joys, longings, and vulnerabilities. Then, lovemaking is truly making love.

Why is sex such a huge issue for dissatisfied partners? Because typically it's the first thing affected when a relationship falters. It's not the true problem, though. What's really happening is that a couple is losing connection; the partners don't feel emotionally safe with one another. That in turn leads to slackening desire and less satisfying sex, which leads to less sex and more hurt feelings, which leads to still looser emotional connection, and around it goes. In short, no safe bond, no sex; no sex, no bond.

The safety of our emotional connection defines our relationship in bed as well as out. Depending on how comfortable we are with closeness and how safe we feel with our loved one, we will have different goals in bed. I call these three kinds of sex *Sealed-Off Sex, Solace Sex,* and *Synchrony Sex.*

SEALED-OFF SEX

In Sealed-Off Sex, the goal is to reduce sexual tension, achieve orgasm, and feel good about our sexual prowess. It happens with those who have never learned to trust and don't want to open up, or who are feeling unsafe with their partners. The focus is on sensation and performance. Bonding with the other person is secondary. This kind of impersonal sex can be toxic in a love relationship. The partner feels used and objectified rather than valued as a person.

SOLACE SEX

Solace Sex occurs when we are seeking reassurance that we are valued and desired; the sex act is just a tagalong. The goal is to alleviate our attachment fears. There is more emotional involvement than in Sealed-Off Sex, but the main emotion directing the sexual dance is anxiety.

Solace Sex often happens when partners are battling Demon Dialogues, and regular, safe, comforting touch—the most basic bonding connection—is missing.

When partners tell me that they cannot be considerate of one another with everyday acts of caring, I worry. When they tell me that they are not making love, I am concerned. But when they tell me that they don't touch, I know they are really in trouble.

SYNCHRONY SEX

Synchrony Sex is when emotional openness and responsiveness, and tender touch and erotic exploration, all come together. This is the way sex is supposed to be. This is the sex that fulfills, satisfies, and connects. When partners have a secure emotional connection, physical intimacy can retain all of this initial ardor and creativity, and then some. Lovers can be tender and playful one moment, fiery and erotic another. Emotional safety shapes physical synchrony, and physical synchrony shapes emotional safety.

Responsiveness outside the bedroom carries over into it. Connected partners can reveal their sexual vulnerabilities and desires without fear of being rejected. Secure, loving partners can relax, let go, and immerse themselves in the pleasure of lovemaking. They can talk openly, without getting embarrassed or offended, about what turns them off or on.

Secure partners can soothe and comfort one another and pull together to overcome unavoidable problems that are never shown in the movies but are part of everybody's life. My experiences have shown me that people can connect and reconnect, falling in love again and again, and that eroticism is essentially play and the ability to let go and surrender to sensation. For this, we need emotional safety.

When experts suggest that only brand-new relationships can offer exciting sex, I think of an older, long-married couple that I know and how they dance the Argentine tango. They are completely present and engaged with one another. Their moves are achingly deliberate, totally playful, and stunningly erotic. They are so attuned and responsive to one another that even though the dance is fluid, improvised, and in the moment, they never miss a beat or a turn, nor step on each other's toes. They move as one, with grace and flair.

CHECKPOINT: Abstinence Makes the Heart Grow Fonder

The best recipe for good sex is a secure relationship where a couple can connect through A.R.E. conversations and tender touch. Even sex therapists concur that the essential building block of a healthy sexual relationship is *non-demand pleasuring.* For this reason, I often suggest to couples that they abstain from making love for a few weeks. With intercourse forbidden, neither partner gets anxious or disappointed, and they can both concentrate, instead, on exploring all the sensations of touching. Getting used to asking for tender touch deepens a couples' bond, and knowing one another's bodies more intimately, what moves and pleases them, becomes a precious part of a couple's *only for you, only with you* connection.

RESOLVING SEXUAL PROBLEMS

Desire naturally waxes and wanes—with events, the seasons, our health—for a thousand reasons. These fluctuations, however, hit a nerve in most of us and, unless we can talk about them openly, can easily spark or heighten relationship problems. Many partners can tolerate infrequent intercourse, but they cannot tolerate feeling that their partners do not desire them.

LET'S GET INTROSPECTIVE:
Journal Exercise

Alone or with your partner, read and respond to the following questions.

In bed with your partner, do you generally feel emotionally safe and connected? What helps you feel this way? When you do not feel this way, how could your partner help you?

PARTNER 1:

....

....

....

....

....

PARTNER 2:

....

....

....

....

....

....

What is your usual sexual style—Sealed-Off Sex, Solace Sex, or Synchrony Sex? In any relationship all three will probably occur sometimes. But if you habitually move into Sealed-Off Sex or Solace Sex, then this tells you something about your sense of safety in your relationship.

PARTNER 1:

....

PARTNER 2:

....

What are your four most important expectations in bed? Think carefully about your answers. Sometimes they are not what we think of first. Partners have told me that their most important expectation after sex was to be held tenderly and caressed gently, but they'd never expressed that desire to their lover.

PARTNER 1:

_____

_____

_____

_____

PARTNER 2:

_____

_____

_____

_____

Do you feel that you do enough touching and holding in your relationship? A single stroke can express connection, comfort, and desire. When would you like to be touched and held more?

PARTNER 1:

....

....

....

....

....

PARTNER 2:

....

....

....

....

....

WORKSHEET: Exploring Your Desires

If you were to write a "Brief Guide for My Lover," what would you put in it? Your guide might include answers to the following questions.

What helps you begin to be open to sex, both emotionally and physically?

Partner 1:

_____

_____

_____

_____

Partner 2:

_____

_____

_____

_____

What turns you on the most before and during lovemaking?

Partner 1:

_____

_____

_____

_____

_____

Partner 2:

_____

_____

_____

_____

_____

How long do you expect pleasuring or foreplay and intercourse to last?

Partner 1:

_____

_____

Partner 2:

_____

_____

What is your preferred position?

Partner 1:

_____

_____

Partner 2:

_____

_____

_____

Do you enjoy fast or slow lovemaking?

Partner 1:

_____

Partner 2:

_____

What is the most stirring way for your lover to move you and stimulate the deepest engagement in lovemaking? Can you ask for this?

Partner 1:

_____

_____

_____

_____

_____

Partner 2:

_____

_____

_____

_____

What makes sex most satisfying for you? (This may not be orgasm or even intercourse.)

Partner 1:

_____

_____

_____

_____

_____

Partner 2:

_____

_____

_____

When do you feel most unsure or uncomfortable during sex?

Partner 1:

_____

_____

_____

Partner 2:

_____

_____

_____

When do you feel closest to your partner?

Partner 1:

_____

_____

_____

Partner 2:

_____

_____

_____

If you can talk about the above with your partner, great. If not, then maybe you can begin a conversation about how hard it is to share this kind of information.

LET'S GET INTROSPECTIVE:
Journal Exercise

When sex isn't working for you physically, what is it that you want to be able to do as a couple? What do you do when sex isn't working for you emotionally? How can your partner help you here? Create a movie scenario of what this would look like on the silver screen, describing the perfect scene. Of course, there's no such thing as perfect, but it gets the conversation going! The scene begins:

If I were perfect in bed, I would _____,

_____

and then you would feel more _____

_____

_____

See if you can share some of your responses. Then tell one another one way in which the other is already sexually perfect for you in bed and out of bed.

WORKSHEET: Exploring Your Desire as a Couple

Can you each think of a time in your relationship when sex was really satisfying? Write a description of this event in as much detail as possible. Share your stories and tell one another what you have learned from listening to these stories.

Partner 1:

_____

_____

_____

_____

_____

Partner 2:

_____

_____

_____

_____

_____

_____

Think of all the ways sex can show up in your relationship. Can it be simply fun, a way of getting close, a straight physical release, a comforting way to deal with stress or upset, a route into romance and escape from the world, an erotic adventure, a place of tender connection, a burst of passion? Do you feel safe experiencing all of these with your lover? What might be a risk that you would like to take in bed?

Can you tell one another the risk and explain how you might respond if things went badly or if things went well?

Partner 1:

The risk I would take in bed:_____

_____

_____

How I would respond to you if things went badly/well:

_____

_____

_____

_____

Partner 2:

The risk I would take in bed: _____

_____

_____

How I would respond to you if things went badly/well:

_____

_____

_____

_____

CHECKPOINT: Forget Perfection

There are no "perfect" lovers. Given this fact, how would you like to be and see yourself as a lover? Can you share this with your partner?

LET'S GET INTROSPECTIVE:
Journal Exercise

How do you each deal with the inevitable times when you want to make love and your partner is not in the mood or is too tired or not aroused? What do you say? This is a sensitive moment for most of us. We teeter on the brink of rejection and hurt. What would have to happen for this kind of sensitive moment to occur and for you to still feel loved and safely connected? How can your partner make this happen?

PARTNER 1:

....

....

....

....

....

PARTNER 2:

....

....

....

....

....

....

Hold These Tight
....

- Safe emotional connection fosters great sex. Great sex creates deeper emotional connection.
- Sex is intimate play and a safe adventure.
- Touch and chemistry link sex and attachment.

·······························

Keeping Your Love Alive

Conversation #7 is built on the understanding that love is a continual process of seeking and losing emotional connection, and reaching out to find it again. The bond of love is a living thing. If we don't attend to it, it naturally begins to wither. In a world that is moving ever faster and requires us to juggle more and more tasks, it is a challenge to be present in the moment and tend to our own and our partner's need for connection. This final conversation asks you to be deliberate and mindful about your love. Moments of deep attachment *are* powerful enough to hold lovers together year after year. I think of our research showing that couples hold on to the satisfaction and happiness they create in EFT sessions, even through highly stressful events.

A.R.E. conversations are the language of love. They shore up the safe haven that is your relationship and nurture your ability to be flexible, to explore, and to keep your love alive and growing. Conversation #7 is a road map for taking your love into the future. The steps entail:

- Recapping and reflecting on the danger points in your relationship where you slide into insecurity and get stuck in Demon Dialogues. This will allow you to figure out detours and shortcuts that lead you back into safe connection.

- Celebrating the positive moments, big and small. This involves, first, reflecting on the moments in your daily lives that foster openness and responsiveness and reinforce your understanding of the positive impact you have on one another, and second, articulating the turning points in your recent relationship history when your love intensified.

- Planning rituals around the moments of separation and reunion in your daily lives in recognition of your bond, support, and responsiveness. These rituals are a way of holding your relationship safe in a distracting and chaotic world.

- Helping one another identify the attachment issues in recurring differences and arguments, and deciding together how to defuse these issues to deliberately create emotional safety and trust. This will allow you to resolve problems without letting hot attachment issues get in the way. I call this the Safety First Strategy: One partner can bring up a problem in softer, less aggressive ways, and the other partner can stay emotionally engaged in the discussion, even if they don't agree with the view that is being presented.

- Creating a Resilient Relationship Story that describes how the two of you have built and are continuing to build a loving bond. It tells how you get stuck in conflict and distance, and how you have learned to repair rifts, reconnect, and forgive hurts. It is a story about falling in love again and again.

- Creating a Future Love Story that outlines what you want your bond to look like five or ten years down the road, and how you would like your partner's help in making the vision a reality.

LET'S GET INTROSPECTIVE:
Journal Exercise

Why is it that we tend to focus on the negative things and fail to give credence to the wins, even the smallest ones, in our lives? You have probably witnessed this phenomenon in your own life. Maybe you harp on the negative email that came from a colleague, completely forgetting the congratulations you received in yesterday's meeting. Your child missing curfew took the air out of the good news about making the dean's list. You feel like a failure for walking most of the 5K instead of celebrating the fact that you got up and did the race at all! The same happens in our relationships—we misfocus our attention from the positive and loving ways we treat one another onto the latest snafu. We don't tell our partners the specific small ways that they touch us with a spontaneous word or gesture and create a sense of belonging. These A.R.E. moments are opportunities to positively reinforce behaviors that connect us and keep us securely attached. This exercise is about celebrating small moments of connection.

See if you can come up with ways to acknowledge and express that you notice the turning points when love suddenly comes into sharper focus. Can you name a key moment in your last rift when your partner made a physical gesture that signaled compassion, even during a Demon Dialogue? For instance, reaching for your hand, handing you a tissue, offering you a glass of water?

PARTNER 1:

_____

_____

_____

_____

_____

_____

PARTNER 2:

_____

_____

_____

_____

_____

_____

During a Demon Dialogue, did your partner speak words of empathy that showed you that you were being actively listened to and heard? For instance, using phrases like "I think I understand," or, "You must feel unimportant when I don't call you from my overnight work trips," or, "I can see how that would offend you."

PARTNER 1:

....

....

....

PARTNER 2:

....

....

....

Can you name some actions or words your partner typically exhibits or says that you think you should validate? Something they do or say that is inherently part of their nature that anchors you in their love? Think about the behaviors that occur habitually, even when stuck in a Demon Dialogue or a darker period, that you could remember to celebrate in order to spark a moment of connection. For instance, does your partner do chores around the house that you take for granted? Is it your partner's way to always have a hot meal ready or make sure the tires are filled with air before a trip, even if you are both angry?

PARTNER 1:

_____

_____

_____

_____

PARTNER 2:

_____

_____

_____

_____

WORKSHEET: Creating Rituals

Rituals are an important part of belonging. They are repeated, intentional ceremonies that recognize a special time or connection. Rituals engage us, emotionally and physically, so that we become riveted to the present moment in a positive way. We habitually kiss children or other loved ones goodbye and hold and greet them when they return. Why not take the time to formally recognize your relationship with your lover in the small gestures that convey the message, *"You matter to me."* Can you help one another design your own bonding rituals, especially recognizing moments of meeting and separation or key times of belonging?

Fill in the blanks to remember the things you used to do to commemorate comings and goings, especially in the early stages of your courtship or relationship.

On our first few dates, I remember that you made me feel important when you greeted me by *(e.g., looking genuinely excited to see me, making me laugh upon saying hello, telling me you liked something I was wearing)*

Partner 1: _____

_____

Partner 2: _____

_____

When I came home from work, you used to acknowledge me by *(e.g. walking to the front door to open it for me, coming in from another room to see me, or yelling from the backyard, "Hello, I'll be right in.")*

Partner 1: _____

_____

Partner 2: _____

_____

Before you left our bed, you used to *(e.g., kiss me on the cheek, whisper "goodbye," hold me)*

Partner 1: _____

_____

Partner 2: _____

_____

When you left for trips, you always *(e.g., left me a short note telling me you'd miss me, called me throughout the day while you were gone, told me you hated to leave me)*

Partner 1: _____

_____

Partner 2: _____

_____

Now that you have remembered that you did have loving rituals, see if you can agree on some of the suggestions below to create or reinstate connective moments together. An idea that one couple shared with me is lighting a candle before bed to signify "connect time," or "heart-to-heart time." This is the time of the evening that they knew they could hold one another and share their softer places—especially sharing the times they felt close or the times they lost their connection. Another couple, after dinner, especially on Fridays, spends at least forty minutes sharing their week, including the ups and downs, all while consciously attempting to support and validate one another and to explore deep emotions.

Each partner can put a check mark next to the suggestions below that they might like. Two check marks indicate agreement. Or use them as inspiration to create your own rituals together.

☐ Regularly and deliberately holding, hugging, and kissing on waking, going to sleep, leaving home, and returning.

☐ Writing letters and leaving short notes for one another, especially when one person is going away or when a couple has come together after a spat or a time of distance.

☐ Participating in spiritual or other rituals together, such as meeting for special family meals, planting the first spring flowers in a family garden, praying or attending religious events.

☐ Creating a personal sharing ritual that is a time just for sharing things and connecting, not for problem-solving or pragmatic discussions.

☐ Arranging a special time just to be together *(e.g., having breakfast in bed without the kids, shifting schedules to eat breakfast together every day, going for a walk or exercise together).*

☐ Maintaining a regular date night, even if only once a month.

☐ Once a year, taking a class together, learning something new, or doing a project together.

☐ Attending to your partner's daily struggles and victories and validating them on a regular basis *(e.g. small comments like, "That was hard for you to do, but you went for it," or, "You worked so hard on that project, no one could have tried harder").*

☐ Taking opportunities to publicly recognize your partner and your relationship. *(e.g., a ceremony, such as a renewal of vows, or it can be a simple thank-you to your partner in front of friends for making a wonderful supper or helping you reach a personal goal).*

Our shared ideas for rituals of separation and reunion:

Separation:

_____

_____

_____

_____

Reunion:

_____

_____

_____

CHECKPOINT: Safety First

Sorting out attachment issues from everyday recurring problems so that the latter can be easily tackled together is a key part of keeping love strong. Couples who practice EFT become skilled at solving the day-to-day problems that plague their relationship. They learn to become cooperative, open, and flexible. This is because mundane problems are now just that. They are no longer the screen on which partners' attachment fears and unmet needs are projected.

Are you aware of the practical problems that play recurring roles in your relationship? Can you identify how they might threaten your newfound commitment to one another? Do you notice if one of these issues still triggers a fear? I encourage couples, as part of their planning for the future, to take an ongoing frustration, such as wanting your partner to be a more involved parent or to be included in your partner's social gatherings, and to have an A.R.E. conversation around the issue, sharing the attachment needs and fears that this topic brings up.

WORKSHEET: Creating a Resilient Relationship Story

We use stories to make sense of our lives. And we use them as models to guide us in the future. We shape stories and then stories shape us. Once partners feel safe with one another, they can create a clear story of their relationship and figure out how to recover from disconnections and make their bond stronger. This not only sums up their past in a way that makes sense, it gives them a blueprint for the future.

Your Resilient Relationship Story should recap how you both have been stuck in insecurity and then found ways to move out of those mires together. In the process of writing your story, you will both reflect on your relationship. It is not uncommon for couples who haven't begun their EFT journey yet to have two very different versions of the relationship, as if they have been living in a different marriage. Now you will be able to create a clear, logical story of how your problems evolved and how you have reclaimed your marriage.

Before you write your story, use the following prompts to help you articulate the various elements.

Three adjectives or images that describe your relationship when it was stalled with insecurity and negative spirals. *(e.g., dead-ended, exhausting, a minefield.)*

_____

_____

_____

Two different verbs that capture how both of you moved in your negative dance and how you were able to change the pattern. *(e.g., I pushed, you turned away, then, but we learned to talk about how scared we were and reached out for one another.)*

_____

_____

_____

One key moment when you saw one another differently, felt new emotions, and were able to reach for one another. *(e.g., I remember that Saturday afternoon when I had walked out. I came back into the room and you were weeping. The look on your face really got to me. I just felt sad and I needed your help. We had to help one another get there.)*

_____

_____

_____

Three adjectives, emotions, or images that express your relationship right now. *(e.g., playful, contented, delighted, blessed, hand in hand)*

_____

_____

_____

One thing you are doing to keep your connection with one another open and growing. *(e.g., cuddling before we fall asleep, kissing when we wake up)*

_____

_____

Now write your story. Don't forget to give it a fantastic title!

TITLE: _____

_____

_____

_____

_____

_____

_____

_____

_____

_____

_____

_____

_____

_____

_____

_____

_____

_____

_____

_____

CHECKPOINT: Holding On to Positive Changes

When you move into new ways of connecting with your partner, it is useful to take the new emotions, perceptions, and responses and integrate them into a narrative that captures all these changes. Your Resilient Relationship Story gives you a coherent way of reflecting on your relationship drama, a drama that is always unfolding no matter how clear your focus. Revisiting your story makes it easier to hold on to the positive changes you've made and gives you a model of your relationship as a safe haven that you build together and can rebuild again.

WORKSHEET: Create a Future Love Story

I now ask partners to make up their Future Love Story. The more of a safe haven we have with our loved one, the more assured, assertive, and adventurous we can 'be. When our loved one is by our side, we tend to have more faith in ourselves and can dream in a new, expansive way. In this story, partners relate their vision of their future relationship. They then ask one another for support and discuss how they can make it a reality together. Consider the following questions to get you started.

What are your personal dreams for the next year? For the next five years?

Partner 1: One year _____

_____

Five years _____

_____

Partner 2: One year _____

_____

Five years _____

_____

How do you envision your relationship in the future? *(e.g., improve our sex life, or maintain certain rituals we've created.)*

Partner 1: _____

_____

Partner 2: _____

_____

When you are very old, what would you like to be your legacy? For example, what would you like to be able to tell your grandchildren about your relationship? Or what photos or other artifacts do you hope your good friends will hold on to? What do these artifacts represent or show?

Partner 1: _____

_____

Partner 2: _____

_____

Now write your story. Have fun giving it a title!

TITLE: _____

_____

_____

_____

_____

_____

_____

_____

_____

_____

_____

_____

_____

Hold These Tight

....

- Reviewing, ritual-making, and story-writing are ways of encouraging couples to continuously pay attention to their relationships.
- Having a strong and lasting love helps partners thrive emotionally and intellectually. We don't need to be rich or smart or funny; we just have to be there, in all senses of the word.
- Love can do more than last—it can flower again and again.

Congratulations! You've just taken a huge step on your journey as a couple. Please visit drsuejohnson.com to find videos, articles, and online courses to further explore how EFT can enhance your relationship. I also invite you to subscribe to my monthly newsletter or visit me on social media.

May you continue to hold one another tight, for a lifetime of love!

 DrSueJohnson

 @Dr_SueJohnson

 DoctorSueJohnson

RESOURCES

....

BOOKS:

Hold Me Tight: Seven Conversations for a Lifetime of Love
Love Sense: The Revolutionary New Science of Romantic Relationships
Created for Connection

ONLINE COURSE:

Hold Me Tight® Online — www.holdmetightonline.com

For more information on all of Dr. Sue Johnson's materials, please visit drsuejohnson.com

NOTES

NOTES

NOTES

NOTES

INDEX

....

ABOUT THE AUTHOR

D R. SUE JOHNSON, a recipient of the Order of Canada, is an internationally recognized leader in the field of couple interventions. A clinical psychologist, Distinguished Research Professor at Alliant International University in San Diego, and professor emeritas with the University of Ottawa, Canada. Dr. Johnson is the primary developer of Emotionally Focused Therapy (EFT) and as the Director of the International Centre for Excellence in Emotionally Focused Therapy (ICEEFT), has trained thousands of therapists in North America and around the world. She is the author of numerous articles and books, including *Hold Me Tight*, *Love Sense*, and *Created for Connection*.

 DrSueJohnson
 @Dr_SueJohnson
 DoctorSueJohnson
drsuejohnson.com

Also available from Dr. Sue Johnson

"The best couples' therapist in the world"

—John Gottman, PhD, bestselling author

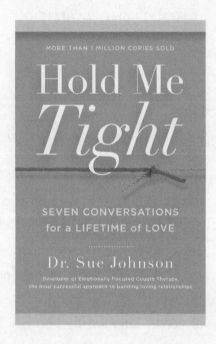

MORE THAN 1 MILLION COPIES SOLD

Hold Me *Tight*

SEVEN CONVERSATIONS
for a LIFETIME of LOVE

Dr. Sue Johnson

Developer of Emotionally Focused Couple Therapy,
the most successful approach to building loving relationships

Hold Me Tight

More than 1 million copies sold

"This fabulous book will be of great benefit to couples trying to find their way to better communication and deeper, more fulfilling ways of being with each other. Bravo!"

—Daniel J. Siegel, M.D., author of *The Whole Brain Child*

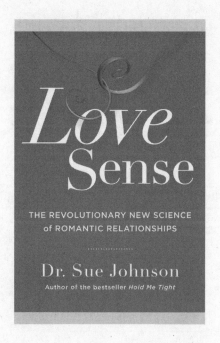

THE REVOLUTIONARY NEW SCIENCE
of ROMANTIC RELATIONSHIPS

Dr. Sue Johnson

Author of the bestseller *Hold Me Tight*

Love Sense

"There is much in *Love Sense* that any couple who has ever felt out of tune will relate to, and good advice for building harmony for the long haul."

— *The Wall Street Journal*

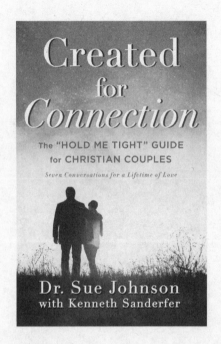

Created for Connection

A groundbreaking and remarkably successful program for creating stronger, more secure relationships not only between partners, but between us and God.